Is it the desire of your heart to see your children and grandchildren follow Jesus? Your home is the number one place of spiritual influence. But you need a plan! This book is packed with creative ways to help your entire family pray and experience God's Word together. I believe this practice of "family worship" will transform your family, for generations to come.

ROB RIENOW
Visionary Family Ministries, www.VisionaryFam.com

This is a unique resource for parents to help them implement family worship. In it you'll learn not only why and how to have family worship, but find a multitude of engaging, interactive lessons for weekly family worship nights. Sergey Sologub has assembled an amazing assortment of stories and activities to help parents teach their children the attributes of God.

DONALD S. WHITNEY
Professor of Biblical Spirituality and associate dean at The Southern Baptist Theological Seminary, Louisville, Kentucky; author of many books, including
Spiritual Disciplines for the Christian Life

I know Sergey as an exuberant, energetic Christian in the troubled country of Ukraine. He understands that accomplishing our mission to change society, and indeed the world, must begin at home. Family devotions used to be a hallmark of faithful families. I hope this winsome and oh-so-practical book helps to revive the practice.

PHILIP YANCEY
Author of numerous books, including *The Bible Jesus Read*

As a father, I remember gathering in the morning with five children of various ages, trying to do family worship in a way that would engage each of them and lay a strong foundation for their own faith and walk with God. Sergey has done just that! By focusing on the alphabet and the attributes of God, he's given us a plan that meets the criteria of keeping it short, making it creative, and focusing on what matters. May God use this tool to stir up young hearts for the glory of God!

BRAD BIGNEY
Pastor, counselor, and author of *Gospel Treason*

This book by Pastor Sergey Sologub is a certain "textbook" for the organization and development of family worship. It will become an interesting, creative, and captivating discovery for the whole family of our great God the Savior. Nowhere else can faith in God be taught and demonstrated better than in the circle of family, among loved ones.

MYKOLA ROMANUK
Lead pastor, Irpin Bible Church (Irpin, Ukraine)

Thank you, Sergey, for bringing the attention of all of us to such an important aspect of life. Very few people write on this subject, and even fewer people suggest practical help, especially from personal experience. The thought and advice found in *Kitchen Table Devotions* have a good biblical foundation and plenty of illustrations from personal life that make the reading of this book interesting and attractive.

KONSTANTIN GONCHAROV
Founding pastor of Irpin Bible Church; missionary in South Florida

The potential of this book is in creating the moments of family worship and practices that allow us to pass our values and faith to the next generation. *Kitchen Table Devotions* can serve the readers as a road map to create their own topics and approaches. The victory for the author of this book will not be the fact that it will be read, but if the reader will have moments spent with the children in worship that will stay with them forever.

YAROSLAV PYZH
President of Ukrainian Baptist Theological Seminary (Lviv, Ukraine)

To be a Christian parent is a special privilege, one that has an important mission, a command from the Lord—to raise children "in the discipline and instruction from the Lord" (Eph. 6:4). You cannot do this without family worship time when the whole family meets around the Word of God and prayer. But how to do it better? How to organize these meetings? What to do during these meetings? This book by Sergey Sologub, *Kitchen Table Devotions*, answers these and many other questions. We already used this book in our family and found it to be useful and practical!

EVGENIY BAKHMUTSKIY
Pastor-teacher, Russian Bible Church (Moscow, Russia)

Amazingly captivating by content and depth, this book by Sergey Sologub is not just worthy of reading but is necessary for each family that wants a true worship to God. I am confident that readers will not be disappointed. And the parents who will apply this book in their everyday life will reap a reward. Glory to God for giving wisdom to those who are willing to share with others with what they receive.

PETR LUNICHKIN
Pastor, Saint-Petersburg Evangelical Church
Director of Light on East mission organization (Saint Petersburg, Russia)

kitchen table devotions

WORSHIPING GOD from A to Z AS A FAMILY

—

SERGEY SOLOGUB

MOODY PUBLISHERS | CHICAGO

Unless otherwise indicated, Scripture quotations are taken from the ESV® Bible (The Holy Bible,
English Standard Version®), copyright © 2001 by Crossway, a publishing ministry of Good News
Publishers. Used by permission. All rights reserved.

Scripture quotations marked (NLT) are taken from the Holy Bible, New Living Translation,
copyright ©1996, 2004, 2015 by Tyndale House Foundation. Used by permission of Tyndale House
Publishers, a division of Tyndale House Ministries, Carol Stream, Illinois 60188. All rights reserved.

All emphasis to Scripture has been added.

Edited by Pamela Joy Pugh
Interior design: Erik M. Peterson
Cover design and illustration by Connie Gabbert
Interior illustrations by Kelsey Fehlberg
Author photo: ChinKar, Singapore

Library of Congress Cataloging-in-Publication Data

Names: Sologub, Sergey, author.
Title: Kitchen table devotions : worshiping God from A-Z as a family /
  Sergey Sologub.
Other titles: 880-01 Abetka pokloninnia v sim'ï. English.
Description: Chicago : Moody Publishers, 2021. | Translation of: Abetka
  pokloninnia v sim'ï. | Includes bibliographical references. |
  Translated from Ukrainian. | Summary: "Kitchen Table Devotions is a
  thoughtful but simple way for parents to creatively teach their children
  about the Lord. Each devotion follows the letters of the alphabet so
  children of all ages can engage. Parents will learn practical guidance
  for how to make this special time part of your family's consistent
  rhythm of life"-- Provided by publisher.
Identifiers: LCCN 2020024292 (print) | LCCN 2020024293 (ebook) | ISBN
  9780802420367 | ISBN 9780802498946 (ebook)
Subjects: LCSH: Families--Prayers and devotions. | Children--Prayers and
  devotions. | Families--Religious life.
Classification: LCC BV255 .S7713 2021 (print) | LCC BV255 (ebook) | DDC
  249--dc23
LC record available at https://lccn.loc.gov/2020024292
LC ebook record available at https://lccn.loc.gov/2020024293

Websites referenced were accurate at the time of the original publication but may have since changed
or ceased to exist. The inclusion of website references does not imply publisher endorsement of the
site's entire contents.

Originally delivered by fleets of horse-drawn wagons, the affordable paperbacks from D. L. Moody's
publishing house resourced the church and served everyday people. Now, after more than 125 years of
publishing and ministry, Moody Publishers' mission remains the same—even if our delivery systems
have changed a bit. For more information on other books (and resources) created from a biblical perspective, go to www.moodypublishers.com or write to:

Moody Publishers
820 N. LaSalle Boulevard
Chicago, IL 60610

1 3 5 7 9 10 8 6 4 2

Printed in the United States of America

To fathers—
that we could rightly and majestically teach our families about God.

To my wife, Tanya—
that she would keep on clinging to God with all of her heart.

To our children, Vladislav, Anna, and Yegor—
that they would think correctly about God.

About the Author

Sergey Sologub came to believe in Jesus Christ in 1995. Seven years later, he married. Together with his wife, Tatiana (Tanya), he lives in a happy marriage, raising three children, Vladislav, Anna, and Yegor. He is a pastor of Irpin Bible Church in the Kiev region, Ukraine. Sergey graduated from the Training Institute for Church Ministers in Irpin, Ukraine, and later graduated with honors from the Ukrainian Baptist Theological Seminary (UBTS) in Lviv. He considers acknowledging God and leading others to know Him to be his life calling.

A Note from the Publisher

This book was originally written in Ukrainian and has been so well received that it has been translated into Russian, German, and Chinese so far, with minimal content adjustments for language and cultural considerations. Moody Publishers is privileged to present the English version to our readers.

Contents

Let's See the Big Picture:
Thanks to . . .

MY HEART IS FULL of thanks:

To **Jesus Christ** for saving me and bringing me into His Father's family, whom I never cease to admire.

To my wife, Tanya, for her love, patience, and daily support in prayers. To my children, Anna, Vladislav, and Yegor, for their encouragement in family worship and for putting up with all my creative experiments. To my mother and mother-in-law for their constant prayers.

To Pastor Gerhard Jan Rotting from Germany for his personal example and dedication in this book's writing. He was my first mentor, who put the importance of writing in my heart when I was young. I am grateful to the leadership of the Christian's Life Center of Ukraine for the time and conditions for writing this book.

To our close partners Jeremy and Cheryl Harbinson and the Minnowburn Trust from Northern Ireland—for their faith in me, as an author, and for their support throughout the book. To my best friend Tyoma Kondrashoff for his loyalty to stay with me, for primary proofreading, and for constant encouragement. To my friend Niall Nixon and his family for faithful praying for the future publication of my first book.

To Michael Cherenkoff and Mission Eurasia team—they found something special in the manuscript and published the first version of this book in Ukraine. They helped me understand the value of this book for families.

To Roman Shpachenko from Ukraine and his family for believing that the English-speaking world needs this book and shared with me not only their heart, but also their finances to translate the text of the manuscript into English. I'm also grateful to translator Konstantin Ivantsov for the excellent translation of the manuscript into English.

To Rachel Schupack for adapting the list of God's attributes to English. To Savannah Chorn for adapting the primary English version of the text. To Cheryl Warner for the first deep edition of the English text.

I am particularly grateful to my American friends Philip and Janet Yancey for their support and for the opportunity to visit the LittWorld 2018 conference, organized by John Maust and MAI's team. At that conference in Singapore I met Randall Payleitner from Moody Publishers (MP) and gave him the very first English version of the book. Later I sent him a first hard copy, printed by Andrey Kravchenko from DigiBooks.

To John Hinkley from MP, for taking over the passion of our first meeting in Chicago. To Pam Pugh, editor from MP, for her final editorial work. To MP board members, who decided to publish this book in English.

To American pastors, who shared their inspiring feedback about this book—Donald S. Whitney, Rob Rienow, and Brad Bigney. Thank you for your support! Without you, this book would not have reached many families.

Getting Started:
A Kitchen Table Theology

IN THE SUMMER OF 2016, we had an incredible opportunity to spend time at the seacoast of the eastern European country of Georgia with friends. It wasn't too difficult for two families to bring some order into our shared vacation time. All of us decided that we would not only sunbathe and go swimming in the Black Sea; we decided that one hour after lunch would be spent in Bible discussions and joint prayer. In our schedule, we called this time "family worship."

"My friends, I believe that God has prepared something very special for us during our vacation," I began. "We will not only rest after lunch, but have an interesting family worship session each day at that time. What do you think?"

The other adults and the children nodded.

"Together we'll learn new things about God, and to help us with that, we will use the alphabet. Today is our first day, and it means that we will start with the letter A. Who can think of a characteristic of God that starts with A?"

Of course, I wasn't expecting every hand to fly up; I myself don't know many characteristics that start with the letter A, though by using this question, I was trying to lead our discussion in a certain direction. But after quite a tiring workout in the seawater followed by a large lunch, all one could focus on was a refreshing nap.

"Author," said one of the adults.

"Thank you! Yes, indeed God is the Author of everything! And what other words starting with the letter A can we call God?"

"Alone," suggested our five-year-old son.

"If you wanted to say that God is the only God, you're definitely right! God alone is God, and there is no other but Him," we agreed.

The adults smiled. Then there was a small pause, for it wasn't very easy to come up with more descriptions of God starting with an A. So I continued, but now with a different question.

"Can you guess how children say the word *dad* here in the country of Georgia?"

My daughter had the answer. "Here they say the word for *mama* when they call their dad! Aunt Zhuzhuna told me that!"

"Yes," I agreed. "*Dad* is actually pronounced like *mama*. But do you know how they say *dad* not far from Georgia—in Turkey, for example? Does anyone know?"

It was obvious that everyone would gladly answer if they knew and that everyone was eager to find out.

"Here's how: when they say *dad*, it is pronounced *baba*!"

Everybody laughed. It was time to hit the target.

"But do you know what Jesus called His Father? Or how this word sounds in His language? He called His Father *Abba*. This is how the word *father* sounds in the ancient Aramaic language! So, *Abba* is the characteristic of God that starts with the letter A that we will be talking about today."

And then I read out loud a passage from Romans:

"For you did not receive the spirit of slavery to fall back into fear, but you have received the Spirit of adoption as sons, by whom we cry 'Abba! Father!'" (Rom. 8:15).

We focused on the fact that we can address the Almighty Lord God with the words *Father* and even the more intimate name *Dad*. Then I told them a story about a president's son. (You'll read about this in Part Two of the book. But stay with me; don't skip ahead!) Then we ended our family worship time with a prayer of thanksgiving that purposefully started with the words, "Our dear heavenly Father . . ."

The next day we listed several characteristics of God that started with the letter B and had a detailed study of one of them: "Beautiful" Lord. This time our children were more active. After a few days, we noticed that even during breakfast the kids were already reminding one another what letter we would discuss that day, and trying to think of qualities of God that started with that letter. The phenomenon, which is known as the formation of "personal theology," i.e., the inner understanding of God, began to take place. And this was happening, mind you, not behind the seminary walls, but at the dining table! Day after day we took one of God's characteristics that started with the letter of the day and studied it together. While our skin was developing a nice suntan, our hearts were growing a majestic new understanding of God. During the next weeks of our vacation, we covered the whole alphabet.

We had a clear plan, and it helped us to move forward in our knowledge of God. This is possible for your family as well. If you let me tell you about it a bit more, this book may become your family's guide to the knowledge of God. It is not a theological textbook, but my own reflections on God based on biblical texts.

Worshiping by alphabet is biblical

"Alphabetical" worship of God did not start with me or with our family. Such worship was born in the Bible, and its authorship belongs to David. It was he who used creativity in his worship of God when he wrote a few of his psalms (or songs) following the alphabet! Psalm 145, for example, is written in such a way that every new line starts with a new letter of the Hebrew alphabet. This form of poetry is called an acrostic. Partial or complete examples of such worshiping in alphabetical order can be found in Psalms 9, 10, 25, 34, 37, 111, 112, and also in the famous and the longest of the psalms, 119, which is written as an acrostic with eight verses given to each letter.

How to best use this book

Contemplating God regularly and constantly is needed in our families and churches. A. W. Tozer put it well:

We must practice the art of long and loving meditation upon
the majesty of God. This will take some effort, for the concept
of majesty has all but disappeared from the human race."[1]

The skill of meditation and contemplation of God indeed requires some effort. Such a habit can't be developed by simply reading a book, and I am well aware of that. Developing a habit of knowing God is a lifelong process. And that's why this book contains both some theory and some practical guidelines.

The first part of the book is more theoretical. It describes biblical principles and our experience of having family worship evenings. It will help you parents communicate the knowledge of God to your children. And imagine, what will your children do when they grow up?

The second part of the book is more practical. It lists twenty-six characteristics of God in alphabetical order. Among them you'll find names of God, figures or images, titles, and actions. You'll also find that these selections can be used for worship in a family or in a group setting.

If you choose to go through this with your family in a letter-a-day format, you'll complete a twenty-six-day marathon of the knowledge of God. You might instead choose to use these once a week either with your family or with a larger group. This way, you'll have six months' worth of weekly meetings to get to know God and His attributes better.

It's time to get started. Chapter 1 will talk about how to put a regular worship time into practice.

PART ONE

THE IMPORTANCE OF FAMILY WORSHIP AND HOW TO MAKE IT HAPPEN

From Wednesdays to Capital Letter Wednesdays

DURING A CERTAIN TIME in our lives we had "guest evenings" on Wednesdays, and we didn't even imagine what it would grow to become in the near future. One night we were expecting our friends to come, and before the meeting we discussed a few details over the phone. "We are really looking forward to seeing you!"

"What should we bring?"

"Bring something for tea, and we'll take care of the rest. We're looking forward to seeing you," I repeated, ending the conversation.

Those guest evenings were always a special time for our family. They were filled with fellowship with other families and opportunities to share our experiences, and they were often concluded with a prayer for one another. We valued these meetings very much, and therefore had them regularly. Having one night a week set aside for guests was helpful for planning other activities during the week. And it was a defining factor in creating another even more important evening activity in our life than the guest evening was.

During one of the meetings, our pastor gave me the book *Visionary Parenting* by Rob Rienow. The author addressed it to fathers, and in it he dealt a lot with a family worship time. Out of everything I read in the book, one paragraph impressed me specifically. The author discussed how his family gathered together once a week at the table and sang. He also mentioned having a Bible study in the family circle. I don't know why, but my whole being just clung to that vision. Perhaps it was because during that time I felt a deficit of such a time in my own family. We had a guest evening every Wednesday, but we didn't have a regular time for spiritual fellowship in the circle of our family. Our souls needed an all-capital-letters WEDNESDAY.

Several days had passed since I read that part of the book, but I couldn't shake off the mental picture of having our family at the table, singing together and experiencing God as closely as if He were sitting right there among us. I reread the paragraph again.

Having bookmarked the page, I started to look for a convenient occasion to share this inspiring picture with my wife, Tanya. Such an opportunity presented itself at supper.

"Sweetheart, I want to share something from the book I'm reading," I said, and read the paragraph out loud.

Then I completed the picture with my own "paint." I suggested how wonderful it could be if we had a special time for worshiping God as a family. And she bought that vision! Now we shared it together. The only small thing left to do was to tell our children. And when a good opportunity came, I tried to do it in a most solemn manner.

"My dear ones! Starting tonight we are going to have a special activity in our family. The Family Evening will be a time when we worship God, sing, pray, and study the Bible together as a family."

So the decision was made and, though our young daughter didn't fully understand what it was all about, she nodded in agreement. It was almost a week until the first night was scheduled. I started to cook up a step-by-step plan for the upcoming evening. How do we fill that time? First, it must include singing together. Immediately I recalled a few verses from the Bible that encourage us to express our worship in song:

Be filled with the Spirit, addressing one another in psalms and
hymns and spiritual songs, singing and making melody to the
Lord with your heart.
—EPHESIANS 5:18–19

Let the word of Christ dwell in you richly, teaching and admon-
ishing one another in all wisdom, singing psalms and hymns
and spiritual songs, with thankfulness in your hearts to God.
—COLOSSIANS 3:16

But there was a tiny problem: I couldn't play the guitar, which would have
been a perfect way to lead the family singing. What to do? Suddenly I had a
thought to use Christian karaoke from the internet. My YouTube search for
"Christian children's songs" brought up a whole bunch of familiar titles. There
was the solution! I selected some songs and created a separate playlist with
them. Then I spent some time preparing a topic for our discussion and thought
about the way I was going to lead the concluding prayer at the table. For the next
few days before the event I was playing the whole scenario in my head over and
over again.

THE FIRST EVENING

The time for our first family evening had finally come. I remember how I was
a bit nervous because I felt like I was going to lead a seminar for other families
instead of spending time with my own. I had my laptop with the selected songs
sitting on the table. We sang the first one, then the second, and then the third.
The singing was quite lively!

"I want to sing one more!" exclaimed our daughter Anna.

"Maybe next time," I replied.

At that moment I was really committed to sticking to the plan I prepared.
I was convinced that one step right or left would ruin the whole thing. It took

months before I learned to be free and joyful in the way I lead our family evenings. After singing, I read a Bible passage and we discussed it together. The passage was taken from the book of Proverbs, and it dealt with bad and good words. I asked questions to my daughter and my wife alike. We were having a good discussion.

"And what should we pray about now?" I asked my "home flock."

The most charming eyes looked at me with intensity. The kids suggested a few items for prayer. We prayed. It was over. When we were going to bed, I asked my wife how she liked our evening time. She said she liked it. Her affirmation meant a lot to me; it meant that we were headed in the right direction.

The next Wednesday came. Again we sang a few songs from YouTube, but this time they were followed by a twenty-minute episode from a Christian puppet show called *Ella's Playground*. This show's episodes are quite dynamic in their content and are geared for children the same age as our daughter. No wonder she liked the video so much! When the episode was over, I opened a passage from the Bible and we read it together to reinforce what we learned from the video. Our family evening was closed with a prayer.

SALVATION FROM THE MONOTONY

In another week we gathered around the table again, and again we sang along with YouTube videos and studied a Bible story, and the evening was concluded with a prayer. After we had had a few such evenings, I started to feel that they were very much alike. We wanted a routine, but not a rut! The way this time was spent was becoming predictable, and the newness of our family evenings threatened to grow into a tradition with a long gray beard. Something inside me was prompting me to rethink the order of our family evenings while still keeping the essence of our common worship of God. But how do we do that in the context of our family? I was perplexed. But by the grace of God I didn't have to wait for the answer very long. My wife was the first one to start on it.

"You do feel that our family evenings for some reason are pretty much alike, don't you?"

"Yes, I've noticed that too," I replied.

"I have a suggestion," she said. "Why don't we change the leader from time to time? We could take turns leading. One week you prepare your 'church service,' and the next week I take my turn in leading the evening." She was right, I did lead these evenings like church services! She continued. "We could cook something together. Our daughter might be in charge for the third week. Let her suggest ideas for our worship time, and let her take a turn leading it."

My wife's words were a huge inspiration for me. This was the remedy for the monotony!

"I like your suggestion," I said. "By rotating the leaders, we can keep the freshness of our family evenings."

Monotony immunity was developed, but there was another issue that kept me in unrest. "Cook something together . . . cook something together . . ." This phrase played over and over in my head, but the voice of tradition was whispering inside me. "Her idea is fine, but it is sort of unspiritual. How can we have a time of spiritual fellowship while cooking something together? It won't be a church service, that's for sure . . ." Until that moment, the ideas of "food" and "worshiping God" had been kept on different shelves in my mind. Every time I tried to combine my thoughts about God and about food, the result was something like, "Don't you dare mix what is sacred with what is profane!" That was the reason why my wife's suggestion to spend a worship evening cooking something together caused me some stress. "Well, it's already decided, so let it be. We'll see how it goes," I told myself, trying to be calm about it.

Maybe for you there's still a huge gap between the words "food" and "worship," and that gap needs to be dealt with in light of the Bible. We'll talk in chapter 6 about blessing God and blessing our food.

COOK SOMETHING TOGETHER

It was time for the family evening that my wife had prepared. I felt it as I was approaching our home. Our kitchen's ventilation grill exits right next to the front door. Oh, what an inviting aroma! The whole evening was special as well.

We were making pizza: the crusts were prebaked, and ingredients for the filling were sliced up, so each one of us could make whatever pizza we liked. The fun of cooking was followed by joyful fellowship at the table. For the first twenty minutes, I entertained the thought of a short sermon that could be delivered at a convenient moment. Now I realize that it would not have made the whole thing any more "spiritual." I was going to learn practically the principle described in the letter to the Corinthians: "So whether you eat or drink, or whatever you do, do it all for the glory of God" (1 Cor. 10:31 NLT).

I already knew how to go to church, pray, or lead a home worship gathering "for the glory of God," but I didn't know how to eat for the same cause! It took time before I was able to learn this by the mercy of God. Now when we sit at the dining table and hold hands, I usually say, "Blessed are You, our Lord, who sent us this food. We worship You, our caring Father. Amen."

When we sit at the table and gobble up flavorful food, we experience a special time together. Food and worshiping God are no longer kept on "different shelves" in my mind. Now everything has its place, just as it was originally designed by the Lord. This is just wonderful: to sit like that as a family in the presence of the holy God and with grateful hearts partake of what He has generously provided us. It was He, our Lord, who gave different tastes and smells and textures to fruits and vegetables. And here, at this table, we see the full cycle of the glory of God as we return it to Him!

It has been four years now, but I still like the way my wife leads our family evenings. A culinary approach is not the only one in her arsenal. We not only partake of the food "for the glory of God," but we also do crafts from time to time when we make something with our hands. My wife and I are learning to understand the second part of the aforementioned principle from 1 Corinthians 10:31: "Whatever you do, do it all for the glory of God."

That night we took a lot of joy in making pizza and in eating it up. While we were still at the table, I turned to Anna.

"Sweetheart, next Wednesday is your turn to prepare our family evening. Do you need any help?"

Her eyes lit up. She asked, "And I'll be able to have it the way I want?"

"Yes," I replied.

"So, you'll be playing the games that I'll have prepared?"

"Uh, of course," I replied with much less enthusiasm.

As you understand, my stereotypes about worshiping God started to break when the ideas of "food" and "worship" ended up on the same shelf. Now it was time to place "games" there as well! I heard the voice of tradition starting up in me, but since we decided to take turns, so be it. Let her lead it, and if there are to be games, we'll play them.

It was the right decision to warn my daughter about the need for advance preparation. She had a whole week ahead to get ready, and during that week she came to me a few times to share her ideas. We selected several games from a book called *Games for Youth Ministry*. The outline was finalized by Wednesday.

FAMILY EVENING THE CHILDREN'S WAY

It was time for the family evening where our daughter was the leader. She gathered us in the living room and said, "We'll have relay races for starters."

We readily accepted the challenge by throwing a ball into an empty toy basket. Whoever gets the ball into the basket the most times wins!

"And now we'll have riddles!" she said. And we started to solve them one by one.

All in all, it was a new experience of a family evening for us, and we concluded it with a good movie. (You can visit PluggedIn.com for a Christian review of movies to see which ones are appropriate for your family.) Speaking of movies . . . a quality discussion about a film will multiply the benefits of watching it. Having a discussion after a film helps us bring up details that we might have skipped. This had been the case for us that time: we watched a film and afterward we discussed the things each of us liked. That evening, like all the previous family evenings, was closed with a unified prayer for one another. We have a red carpet in our room, and every single family evening—whether it was studying the Bible, watching a film, cooking together, or playing relay races—was finished with a prayer on that carpet. So it was that time too: I asked everyone to express their needs and pray.

DIVERSITY OF CLOSING PRAYERS

The closing prayer is a special element of our family worship evenings. We try to be creative about it each time.

- Sometimes we select one of God's attributes (for instance, the one we have been contemplating during the Bible study or while watching a film). Then we worship God while expressing our thoughts about that attribute in our prayer to Him.
- Sometimes I ask, "What do you feel especially grateful to God for this week?" As we recollect, we share how God has been active in our lives, and then we pray with thanksgiving.
- Other times I may ask, "What are your goals and needs for the coming week?" And we share our expectations and then bring them to God in our requests.
- Sometimes our prayer is done according to announcements, where each one of us expresses his or her needs, and as soon as one need is expressed, we decide who is going to pray for it. As it turns out, even when our boy Yegor was just five, he had needs that he wanted us to pray for. One of the parents may pray for them, and the children may pray for the parents' needs.

Prayer helps to develop solidarity in our family. My role as a husband and a pastor in my family is to help my family members strengthen their relationship with God. Children's participation in the family prayer is one way to achieve that. But we don't force our children to pray; rather, we offer them an opportunity to do so. By forcing I mean phrases like, "Now it's Anna's turn to pray," or "Yegor, you will pray." Usually we say, "Who would like to pray?" It is a subtle but very important point, as it implies their personal choice from the heart.

CHILDREN'S EVENING THE GROWN-UP WAY

It was our youngest son's turn to lead our family evening for the first time. The idea that he came up with was just brilliant.

"It's going to be my family evening, so all of us will go to McDonald's!" Simplicity is the ultimate sophistication! He decided not to burden himself with a long preparation. The answer had popped up in his head a week ago. And to him it was clear that Daddy should support his idea. To be frank, I liked the direction the whole thing was taking. And yet, I had to break another stereotype in my head: worshiping God with a Big Mac and Coke—it can't even be possible, can it? (Now, don't put this book aside! In subsequent chapters we will put on our "biblical glasses" and critically reconsider the experience.) A calm atmosphere at the dining table at home is one thing, but is it possible to have a spiritual time with the family in the lively and noisy atmosphere of a fast-food restaurant?

When we went to McDonald's, we gave our order and waited for a good spot to free up. It was crucial to find a quiet nook, as the purpose of our visit was more than just having a bite. We came here to worship God and spend our family evening in fellowship. The ambient noise didn't hinder us from holding hands and praising the Creator. "Blessed are You, our Lord, who sent us finances and an opportunity to eat here. Amen."

"Amen," echoed the rest of the family. Both the food and the fellowship were wonderful. Understanding the importance of keeping the thread of our conversation about God going in a noisy surrounding, I decided to talk about the design of our tongue. We remembered our five basic tastes—sweet, salty, sour, bitter, umami (savory)—and it was a wonderful ground to think about our marvelous Creator who came up with all these and to praise Him together.

Instruction is always the responsibility of the parents. The Bible is very clear on that. Deuteronomy 6 can confidently be called the Biblical Constitution of raising children:

> "These words that I command you today shall be on your heart.
> You shall teach them diligently to your children, and shall talk

of them when you sit in your house, and when you walk by the
way, and when you lie down, and when you rise."
—DEUTERONOMY 6:6–7

The phrase rendered as "teach diligently" means in the original "to focus, to
remind constantly." Spiritual rearing is similar to having to repeatedly sharpen
a pencil because it will lose its sharpness. For example, once children learn the
biblical truth "Do not tell lies," they need to be reminded over and over again for
it to become a part of their character and their lives.

The Bible passage listed above contains a few other important commands for
parents. Let us notice:

- There are places where we need to remind our children of God.
  "In your house"—this is a place where "all masks have slipped."
  At home, we are who we really are. Parents' lifestyles teach
  children much more efficiently than their words. "Walk by the
  way"—this is to say that instruction is equally important both
  at home and beyond, wherever we find ourselves and wherever
  we go about our business. The general meaning of these words is
  "remind them of God in any place."
- There are certain times when children should be reminded of
  God. The words "when you lie down, and when you rise" literally
  mean "day and night." The general meaning of these words is
  "remind them of God at any time."

Instructing children should be done at any opportunity, and even a dinner in
a noisy McDonald's restaurant isn't an exception to this command from God.

Our visit to McDonald's was repeated a few more times, but it wasn't the only
thing in our son's arsenal. One time he suggested going to feed pigeons. That
idea seemed just wonderful! Prior to that, we had fed pigeons at one of the city's
central squares on several occasions. This time, as the times before, we went to a
store and bought a few packets of sunflower seeds.

When they spotted the first seeds dropped on the asphalt, pigeons one by one began to flock around the place where we fed them. Usually the whole process lasts as long as we have seeds, so we buy several big bags. Sometimes these birds come so close that they can literally peck from one's hands. I enjoy watching them surround my son. He is afraid to make even the slightest move, and he throws seeds to his feet in small batches.

More and more pigeons fly closer. In most cases they sit on roofs of multistory buildings, but having noticed their cousins' active movements, they begin to flock together. Sometimes there can be more than fifty of them!

That day, while we were watching the pigeons, we got to talk about church planting. There is quite a similarity between feeding pigeons and planting a new church. I told my children that our Irpin Bible Church, too, once started as a small group of people. God's Word is spiritual food, and those souls "hungry for God" not only found food for themselves at IBC, but those individuals also began to invite their friends to church services. The church started to grow, and it has kept on growing even now. While standing on that square and feeding pigeons, we were talking about God, who builds His kingdom with born-again people. We were giving names to new pigeons that flew closer, and we watched their behavior.

"See how timid this one is!" Anna noticed, pointing to a pigeon that just flew up and gently pecked at the scattered seeds some distance away from the main cluster of birds.

"Daddy, look, this one has a sick foot," said Yegor, pointing to a dark pigeon that drew up his foot while pecking with caution.

"This is what may happen in a church, too. Sometimes there are wounded people who come, but through the fellowship and the Word of God, they receive support and healing from their wounds," I said, recalling a story of a guy I knew whose life God has radically transformed. When Sasha got into a Christian rehabilitation center, he had head trauma. Just like the pigeon with a drawn-up foot, Sasha was looking for help and support from Christians. After some time, his wound was healed, and he came to believe in Jesus Christ. When he returned to his village, Sasha went to the local school and admitted that it was he who had stolen computers from the IT classroom the summer before. He was willing to work out their cost by doing the repairs that were planned for the summer, but the school headmaster told Sasha that he had forgiven him and was happy that Sasha's life had changed. "Stay firm on this way," he told Sasha.

While glancing at the wounded pigeon, the children pondered the story I told them. Together we rejoiced at the miracle of that transformed life.

Sometimes sparrows fly close to pigeons. They tend to stick together as a separate band. Pigeons are larger, and they dominate, leaving only crumbs to sparrows. That observation provided an opportunity for a discussion about new people in a church community. New people find it difficult to join a church where "locals" pay no attention to them.

When we ran out of seeds, the pigeons stayed near us for some time, and then they left our "community," one by one. When I noticed that, I remember telling my children, "When a church ceases to preach the living Word of God and care for people, people will leave that church sooner or later. This is why it is important to pay attention to people so that our love and care for them does not grow weak."

From time to time we go to the park to feed the pigeons. This not only inspires children to take care of God's creation, but also provides a good opportunity to talk about spiritual truths. What does God think about our conversations in which ordinary things acquire a spiritual dimension? I guess God likes it a lot. Even Jesus Christ Himself skillfully turned His observation of birds into lessons on the kingdom of God! And when His gaze fell upon the lilies, people around Him heard truths about God's care (see Matt. 6:26–29). I am convinced that even today the Holy Spirit still gives parents wisdom to enable them to use life situations in instructing their children in faith.

CHAPTER 2

God and Worshiping Him

WE HAVE TALKED A LOT about some practical and creative ways of worship, but now it is time to get to the heart of the matter. What is the nature of worshiping God? In 1920 a famous strongman known as Kid Dundee lifted a barbell that weighed 1,454 kilograms (about 3,200 pounds)—roughly the same weight as the original Volkswagen Beetle with passengers! How would you have reacted if you had been near that strongman in that moment? Perhaps you would have been astonished, and that overwhelming feeling would have burst out as "Wow! This is unbelievable!"

This is the way a human being is designed. Humans are impressed with superiority, and we hasten to express it in words or emotions. This example helps us understand what worshiping God is in its essence.

WORSHIP IS A REACTION TO GOD

God is enormous. God is grandiose. God is impressive. God is mighty and kind beyond measure. No creature can look at God indifferently. It is impossible to come into God's presence and not be amazed, and this is why what surrounds God is called, in the Bible, the "glory of God." I like the definition of God's glory given by the authors of the book *Cat & Dog Theology*:

God's glory is defined as any revelation or expression of His excellency in His presence, creativity, and/or character. [2]

Therefore, the natural reaction to God and His glory is what we call "worship." Reflecting on worship as the chief end of man, Ron Man makes an interesting summary:

> We must learn to cherish God's glory. And to cherish God's glory is what it means to worship. Worship is expressed in many different ways, but in its broadest understanding it comes down to cherishing the glory of God. [3]

It is important to understand that worship is something that is inside a person, coming from the state of one's heart. And it inevitably seeks to come out by expressing itself in various forms: in trembling veneration, in singing, in a joyful spirit, in a pious attitude toward people, work, school, and so on. [4]

This sequence "from the inside out" can be clearly seen in the story of Moses's worship:

> Moses said, "Please show me your glory." . . . The LORD descended in the cloud and stood with him there, and proclaimed the name of the LORD. The LORD passed before him and proclaimed, "The LORD, the LORD, a God merciful and gracious, slow to anger, and abounding in steadfast love and faithfulness, keeping steadfast love for thousands, forgiving iniquity and transgression and sin, but who will by no means clear the guilty, visiting the iniquity of the fathers on the children and the children's children, to the third and the fourth generation." And Moses quickly bowed his head toward the earth and worshiped.
> —EXODUS 33:18; 34:5–8

Moses asks God to show him His glory. And in response God tells him about Himself. In other words, God gives Moses a revelation of Himself. Please take note of a very clear sequence: God reveals Himself. Moses bows down and prostrates himself in worship. This leads us to another very important conclusion.

REVELATION OF GOD INEVITABLY RESULTS IN WORSHIP

Why is this conclusion so important in our reflection? Because it helps us to answer the question, "How do we pass on the worship of God to our children?" From the experience of our family that was described earlier in the book, one can falsely assume that worship of God can be communicated and passed along once you begin to have regular family evenings. This is not so. You may pass along to your children a religious practice or a good habit, but this is a "shell," not the essence.

Worship of God is subtle and evasive. It cannot be "copied" and then "pasted" into other people's hearts. It comes only personally, as a person's response to the revelation of God Himself. And that is why we can confidently say that regular family meetings serve only as a plate that holds the food, i.e., revelation of God taken from the Bible. When children hear their parents share stories about God, they will be impressed by Him, and it will be expressed in their worship.

That is why in the second part of this book you will find descriptions of God's attributes based on the Bible. Using simple examples provided for each attribute, you can become a missionary to your children and pass to them bits of God's glory day by day. The best thing you as parents can do for the spiritual life of your children is provide them with opportunities to go on a "date with God in the Bible's pages," and then encourage them to follow God's revelation. Regular family worship times are good opportunities for such dates with God.

PERMANENT IMPERMANENCE

We have already said that family gatherings can be accompanied by various forms of worship. Worshiping God at the table? Worshiping God in a fast-food restaurant? Worshiping God in the forest? You can come up with a lot of ideas!

Which forms of worship are pleasing to God today? You'll find numerous opinions, but it is only biblical understanding that helps us not to throw the baby out with the bathwater, so to speak. It is quite easy to have a fun and entertaining family evening, but will Jesus eat with you, and you with Him, during that time? (see Rev. 3:20) We as parents need to know the key truths of worship theology in order to base our practice on the Bible, and not on someone else's experience. I hope that a little reflection below will be helpful.

HOW SHOULD GOD BE WORSHIPED?
A THEOLOGY OF FAMILY WORSHIP

God may be worshiped only on His own terms, so let us speak about the boundaries of worship. The Lord gave the children of Israel clear instructions in regard to worship:

- Concerning the time of worship: "Three times a year you shall keep a feast to me."—Exodus 23:14.
- Concerning specific places of worship, He says of the dwelling place of the Lord: "There you shall eat before the LORD your God, and you shall rejoice, you and your households, in all that you undertake, in which the LORD your God has blessed you."—Deuteronomy 12:7. Here the Lord was telling His people to stay away from places that had been dedicated to false, pagan gods. His people were to have nothing to do with any of these, and they must not mix up their worship of the true God with any others.
- Concerning specific actions: "Now on the tenth day of this seventh month is the Day of Atonement. It shall be for you a time of holy convocation, and you shall afflict yourselves and present a food offering to the LORD. And you shall not do any work on that very day, for it is a Day of Atonement, to make atonement for you before the LORD your God."—Leviticus 23:27–28.

God's commandments concerning worship were specific and clear. Their violation could cost the offender his or her inclusion in the community:

> "If anyone who is clean and is not on a journey fails to keep the
> Passover, that person shall be cut off from his people because
> he did not bring the LORD's offering at its appointed time."
> —NUMBERS 9:13

I am convinced that today as well we need clear biblical criteria for worship of God. We cannot build our worship of God on the basis of someone else's experience or information from the books we read, including this one. A. W. Tozer spoke interestingly on this matter: "Look at Cain. Cain had a religious experience, but God did not accept him. Look at Balaam, son of Beor. He had an experience and yet God was not pleased with him."[5]

You and I need to come to understand worship as it is defined by God Himself. For the children of Israel everything was laid out, but now that Christ has come, we are in the church, or New Testament era, and we no longer have the same directives of times and places. We as parents must examine today's criteria for worship. First of all, let us turn to what Jesus Himself said about worship:

> "The hour is coming, and is now here, when the true worshipers
> will worship the Father in spirit and truth, for the Father is
> seeking such people to worship him. God is spirit, and those
> who worship him must worship in spirit and truth."
> —JOHN 4:23–24

Jesus said that God the Father is looking for people whose whole hearts worship Him. He told the woman at the well that specific places—such as the mountain or the temple—are no longer what define worship! So, what is important now? Worship "in spirit" and "in truth" are two of God's criteria for worship. What do these words mean?

Worship in spirit

Spiritual regeneration is the first aspect of worshiping in spirit. Only a regenerated person can worship his or her Creator in the way that is pleasing to God. This is what Tozer says of it:

> Worship is not simply having a solemn feeling about the length
> of time and the brief duration of our lives on earth and the
> vastness of the heavens and the smallness of our bodies. That
> may be beautiful, but it's not worship. To worship acceptably, I
> repeat, is to be born anew by the Holy Ghost through faith in
> the Lord Jesus Christ and have the Holy Spirit of Christ teach
> us to worship and enable us to worship.[6]

Next, "worship in spirit" means the action started in us by the Holy Spirit. As a response to the Word of God, He prompts us to react to the truth with our voluntary worship. This is how theologian Donald Whitney put it: "Having the Holy Spirit residing within does not guarantee that we always *will* worship in spirit and truth, but it does mean we *can*. To worship God in spirit involves worship from the inside out."[7]

Worship in truth

The second criterion of worship that Jesus spoke about is worship "in truth." Again, here's how Donald Whitney expresses it:

> The balance to worshiping in spirit is to worship in truth. Wor-
> ship in truth is worship according to the truth of Scripture. First,
> we worship God as He is revealed in the Bible, not as we might
> want Him to be. We worship Him according to the truth of
> who He says He is: a God of both mercy and justice, of love and
> wrath, who both welcomes into heaven and condemns into hell.[8]

If we do not worship in response to the truth of who God is, our worship is in vain. In contrast to commands given to the children of Israel, there are no detailed descriptions for us as Christians as to the when and where and how of worship. Jesus did not leave us any particular form of worship. He didn't say, "Pray only on your knees," or "Say only these words." Even the prayer He gave us, the Lord's Prayer, is a guide, not an exact prayer to be recited verbatim repeatedly. For example, this prayer does not include words of gratitude to God, though thankfulness is certainly an aspect of prayer (see 1 Thess. 5:18 and 1 Tim. 2:1, for example).

As we have noted, the criteria left by Jesus—"in spirit and in truth"—are more concerned with the very essence of the way God is to be worshiped. Jesus speaks about the worshiper's heart submitted to and bowed down before the Lord. It is from such a heart that the true worship of God starts here on earth. And it is where worship at the dining table begins.

How can God be worshiped today?

So let's consider this: "What forms of worship are pleasing to Him today?" The study of two passages from the Bible will be helpful in finding a more specific answer. These two passages deal with worship in heaven. In the book of Isaiah, we are introduced to heavenly worshipers. In his vision, Isaiah saw the Lord seated on a high throne. Around the throne he saw heavenly beings, seraphim. They loudly glorified God, saying,

> "Holy, holy, holy is the LORD of hosts;
> the whole earth is full of his glory!"
> —ISAIAH 6:3

We are presented with a majestic picture of worship of the Almighty. Their worship is not automatic. I suppose that seraphim utter their words sincerely, from the bottom of their hearts. They looked up to God, saw something special in Him, something that they had not seen before, and their reaction to the glory of God was worship. Then they look at Him again, and there is a new discovery followed by worship!

In the time when everything was rather gloomy in the land of Israel where

Isaiah lived (their king had just died, and the nation was in turmoil), the seraphim cried out, "The whole earth is full of his glory!" Seraphim are able to view earth from the perspective of heaven. No matter what happens on earth, there is constant praise and worship at the throne of God!

Now let's compare another passage with the previous one. In the book of Revelation, the apostle John also sees different creatures before the throne of God. There are some things that sound familiar in their words, and we also learn something new. These creatures constantly cry out saying,

> "Holy, holy, holy is the Lord God Almighty,
> who was and is and is to come!"
> —REVELATION 4:8

Note the first part of that doxology, "Holy, holy, holy is the Lord." These are the very same words that were uttered seven hundred years before in the days of Isaiah! Does that surprise you? Here on earth, generations had replaced generations, multiple wars and disasters had passed, but despite all of this, God continues to be glorified in heaven in the same manner. We might call this "unchangeable worship." But the second part of their prayers changed. The second part of their doxology may be called "relevant worship," and it is something changeable depending on circumstances.

UNCHANGEABLE WORSHIP	RELEVANT WORSHIP
Holy, holy, holy is the Lord	of hosts; the whole earth is full of his glory!
Holy, holy, holy is the Lord	God Almighty, who was and is and is to come!

This study helped us discover the principle of "permanent impermanence." Now we will discuss its practical application.

For example, in our prayer at the dining table, these words may be constant: "Blessed are You, our Lord, who sent us this food . . ." And following this constant part of the prayer, we may add something specific such as, "Thank You for giving us this rice and salad," thus making our worship "relevant." This is how our children thank God in prayer for food; their prayers are relevant every single time, and they will not fit any other lunch or dinner! I enjoy learning it from them.

In this chapter we have learned that worship of God should be done "in spirit and in truth," and it may contain permanent elements and elements that change depending on our current situation.

What should not be missed (permanent)

In family worship evenings, some things are going to change, but there are certain things that need to remain unchanged. In our family we have identified several elements that should never be missed (as you have guessed, these are practical applications from the first column of the table above). This list can be called "the permanent values of family worship."

> *Praising God.* We will praise God every time regardless of who leads the evening or what form the evening takes.
> *A portion of God's Word.* Whether we go to McDonald's, or to the forest, or anywhere else, it is important for me as a father and a priest in my family to take care of accompanying this time with a truth from the Bible.
> *Prayer for each other.* As it was described in the previous chapter, we try to close our evenings with prayer, regardless of the evening's agenda.

I hope that you have accepted this challenge: parents need special wisdom every time to be able to intertwine their fun time with a portion of the Scriptures and prayer. Remember what we have been talking about: "You shall teach them diligently to your children, and shall talk of them when you sit in your house, and when you walk by the way, and when you lie down, and when you rise" (Deut. 6:7).

Praise, the Word of God, and prayer will make family worship evenings deeper and more meaningful.

What can change (impermanent)

Considering the second column of the chart, it should be mentioned that parents need wisdom and creativity to make the family time of worshiping God vibrant and unique. It is uniqueness that makes this time desirable and anticipated. Use different forms of prayers and different ways of communicating the truth. For example, in our Bible study, we use the following creative approaches:

- Read the passage by characters or perform a skit.
- *Draw Bible stories on paper.* Recently we asked our children to draw how they imagine the world of Adam and Eve would be today had they not fallen. The children created wonderful drawings!
- *Watch a video clip on the subject of the passage.* YouTube.com can be helpful to find these. During one of the evenings, we watched a clip about the Ark of the Covenant (from a film about David). Prior to that, our younger son, whenever he heard of an ark, always asked, "Dad, is this the same ark where Noah had all those animals, or is it a different one?" After he saw the Ark of the Covenant with its poles, everything fell into place, and it helped us read the story from 2 Samuel 6 without any stress.
- Make a suitable origami or other craft to illustrate the point.

A creative approach is a vivid part of the agenda, the "relevant worship." Summing up, we should note that in the practice of family worship evenings, it's a good idea to adhere to the model that we call "permanent impermanence." Make every family worship evening creative and special while keeping its main essence—worship of God.

CHAPTER 3

Battle for Family Worship

EVERY TIME YOU MAKE a strong decision to worship God as a family, be ready to fight for that time!

From the very beginning, we set aside Wednesday evenings for our family worship. Wednesday is the middle of the week, a pinnacle of different activities, and no wonder that after a while, our family evening was brutally attacked by ever-increasing busyness. Our church ministers decided to move the pastoral and leadership meetings to Wednesday evenings. Being one of the church pastors, I had to attend. The family time was under attack, and during our family council, we decided to move our family evening to Thursday. As soon as we had adjusted to this shift, I got a phone call:

"We want to remind you that this coming Thursday evening we are having the camp leadership meeting at seven o'clock. You will be teaching one of the topics during the camp, won't you?"

"Yes, I was invited to teach a topic during the camp, but I won't be able to come to the meeting this Thursday," I replied.

"But this is extremely important; the whole camp team is going to be there."

"Yes, I understand, and I'm sorry. But I won't be able to come."

"That is too bad. We'll be looking forward to seeing you the following Thursday, then," the caller said.

"I won't be able to come the following Thursday, either. I won't be able to come on Thursdays at all. I have an appointment that I can't reschedule because all other evenings are already taken."

"What kind of appointment is it that takes place every Thursday?"

"It's a meeting with very important people," I said, and then added, "my family."

I felt a lack of understanding from the other side of the phone line, but I was absolutely serious. Having a strong conviction to be primarily committed to my home flock, I nevertheless found it difficult to say no to matters of the church ministry. Leaping ahead, I should say that I did go to the camp, but I needed to keep on looking for windows in my schedule to delve into the preparation process. But our Thursday evening remained safe under the secure protection of our "no interruptions" policy.

It's important to remember that the battle for worship of God has been going on for ages. Since the fall of Satan our enemy, he has been attacking the worship of God. Here are two examples from Scripture.

The prophet Jeremiah describes the time of the destruction of Jerusalem, noting one important detail—above all, the robbers sought to destroy and desecrate the temple, the holy place of worship: "The enemy has stretched out his hands over all her precious things; for she has seen the nations enter her sanctuary, those whom you forbade to enter your congregation" (Lam. 1:10).

Once the core of the nation (worship of God) is snatched, breaking all the rest will not amount to much. This stays true in regard to an individual, and to his family.

Later, after the ruined temple had been rebuilt, the devil attacked again! Nehemiah, exiled from his homeland and now cupbearer to the king of Persia, learned of the poor condition of Jerusalem. He gained permission and help from the king to repair the walls of the city, and was appointed governor of Judah (which was under Persian control).

Nehemiah returned to Persia to resume his service to the king, and some time after that returned to Jerusalem. He describes what he saw at the temple when he arrived: "I . . . came to Jerusalem, and I then discovered the evil that

Eliashib had done for Tobiah, preparing for him a chamber in the courts of the house of God" (Neh. 13:7).

Just as soon as the leader Nehemiah left the city, the priest provided rooms in the temple as lodging to his relative Tobiah, who was a bitter enemy of Israel! Throughout the whole account of Nehemiah, Tobiah constantly did what he could to disrupt the work of the people of Jerusalem to repair the walls of the city. Did Tobiah need housing? No, he belonged to nobility. That act could not have been seen as anything other than desecration of the temple. And indeed it was so; in subsequent verses we read that it caused people to stumble. To them the temple ceased to be a place of worship. They quit bringing their offerings to God. Levites dispersed to their fields, and the music of worship in the temple was stilled. By prompting Tobiah to lodge in the temple, the devil stole the worship of God. As soon as Nehemiah got back, he threw Tobiah's belongings out of the temple's vault. (Tobiah was lucky not to be seen by Nehemiah!) Worship of God in the temple was restored.

You too are going to fight a battle for family worship. Sometimes you'll have to fight against outside distractions, but at times it will even be church activities that you'll have to choose not to participate in. On one occasion I heard our administrator tell someone about me, "It's no use to invite him anywhere on Thursdays; that's when he has a family evening. He won't go anywhere." I was pleased. One can call it training by constancy, and it was exactly what had taken place there. We discovered an important principle: "Constancy develops the schedule."

Constancy is when your friends know that your Thursday is the family worship evening. Of course, it doesn't exclude a possibility of paying our friends a visit; that is when our families can worship God together. Several times we decided to visit certain families on Thursdays as there were no other opportunities. But as I said before, there are three constant values that we try to instill in our time spent with or as guests: worship of God, a portion of Scripture, and prayer.

WHY IS IT IMPORTANT TO SET TIME ASIDE?

From time to time I come across objections like this one: "I do spend time with my family during the week, so why do we need to set any extra time aside for worship?" Let me share a few real-life examples to illustrate why in our family we allocated a separate evening for family worship.

First, constancy spells value. If your family members see that you have started to have this family time of worship but then you quit or always move it to some other time to make room for other activities, what will it communicate to them? Only one thing will be clear: that such time is of little importance. It's better to keep the pace of regularity than preach to the wind about the importance of family worship.

Once you've allotted such time and told others about it, you have protected that time. Now it's much more difficult for others to try to schedule you for other things during this time.

And this is the time to become closer with your family. In our Slavic culture, we have an acute shortage of time spent with the family. Sunday is a day for church services and different church activities, and Saturday is more for shopping at the market and cleaning around the house than for spending time with one's family. This cannot be said, for instance, of Jewish culture, where Sabbath is the time with the family.

Family worship is the time to express one's gratitude to God and to thank one another in a special way. In a Jewish family the time of the Sabbath fellowship begins with words of praise. The husband praises and blesses his wife before everyone, and then his children. We take great joy in borrowing that tradition, and during our family dinner, I try to remember and remark on the works of my wife from the past week. Then I praise our children. Then Tanya takes a turn in praising, and then our children have a turn to speak. This "bouquet of praises" is concluded with our gratitude to the Lord who gives us strength to live a changed life.

CHAPTER 4

Be Missionaries to Your Children

The next part of the book is designed to help you become missionaries to your children. We tend to think that we must "proclaim the excellencies" of God to other nations, but who said that this passage doesn't relate to our own families?

> But you are a chosen race, a royal priesthood, a holy nation,
> a people for his own possession, that you may proclaim the
> excellencies of him who called you out of darkness into his
> marvelous light.
> —1 PETER 2:9

Isn't it the children in our own families who need to be the first to learn about God's wonderful deeds? Parents have a responsibility in their families to communicate God's excellence into the "culture" of their children. In order to saturate ourselves with the idea of missionary work in our families, let us refresh our minds as to what a missionary is.

A missionary is a Christian who communicates the good news to people in an understandable form. Outside their home country, each missionary encounters cultural barriers. People missionaries seek to reach may have different customs, different history, or a different worldview. Sometimes missionaries face a challenging task to convey the news about a saving God in a manner their audience can appreciate. How is it achieved? One of the ways to do that is to find analogies in the people's culture and use them as parallels to explain truths about God and salvation.

Marilyn Laszlo and her fellow missionary Judy Rehberg went to take the gospel to the Hauna people in Papua New Guinea. They learned that the word for doctor in the language of the people meant "spitter," because when treating a sick person, the medicine man would chew up herbs and healing plants and spit them on the part of the body that was afflicted. When Marilyn and Judy taught them about how Jesus healed a blind man by spitting in the dirt and placing the mud on the man's eyes, the people concluded, "Jesus is the most powerful Spitter in the world!"[9] The missionaries also learned that in this language, the throat is the center of a person's essence, similar to the way we talk about the heart. While we might say, "I have accepted Jesus in my heart," in this language, the missionaries told the people they needed to "ask Jesus into your throat."[10]

In these ways, they helped people understand the gospel of the Lord Jesus by using relevant words and symbols from their own culture. Many missionaries refer to this practice as *redemptive analogies*. Veteran missionary Don Richardson believed that the Lord has already planted the concept of a supreme God into societies around the world, though spiritual understanding may lie dormant for generations. He explained that an unreached people need not deny their cultural background to convert, but once some have converted, these believers will find ways to share the gospel with others in their society, using insight from both Scripture and their own heritage.

The Yali tribe of Western New Guinea, now part of Indonesia, were an especially fierce people who had martyred two missionaries in the mid-1960s. Could a redemptive analogy be found for them?

Don Richardson set out with a partner to learn about the beliefs and customs of this intractable people, searching for an analogy in their culture that would make the gospel clear to them. One day a young Yali told the two men a story about his brother and a friend.

"Long ago, my brother Sunahan and a friend named Kahalek were ambushed by enemies from across the river," the young man recalled. The friend was killed, but his brother Sunahan escaped, darting inside a circular wall made of stone. From there he bared his chest, defiantly mocking his enemies. His assailants put away their weapons and ran.

Don asked in astonishment, "Why didn't they kill him?"

The young man explained. "If they had shed one drop of my brother's blood while he stood within that sacred stone wall—we call it an *osuwa*—their own people would have killed them."

At last, Yali believers and missionaries working with them had a tool to use to apply the gospel to their culture. Who is the perfect *Osuwa*? Jesus Christ, the place of refuge. Embedded within the Yali culture is the instinct that mankind needs a place of refuge, a key teaching of Christianity. Many years before the missionaries arrived, the Yali had constructed a network of these *osuwa* in locations at which most of their fighting took place. Missionaries had seen the stone walls but had not known of their meaning. Now they could relate the *osuwa* to Christ.[11]

The missionaries in this story found in the culture of Yali people an analogy they used to bring them the truth about God in an understandable way. We as parents are missionaries to our own families. We are called to convey the truth about God to our children in a way they can appreciate, helping them to discover the Creator daily.

Now, we just said that "a missionary is a Christian who communicates the good news to people in an understandable form," and you read interesting examples of missionaries who did this in a country far from their own and in a far different culture. Even when we're in our own country, we need to communicate truth in a way our children can grasp and remember.

So now the question is: "How do we do it in an understandable way?" You'll see why, along with each of the attributes of God, there's a story or a parable or another way to illustrate the truth. I hope that these will serve as a good springboard to help you understand the given biblical verses about God, and to help you explain them to your children.

PART TWO

26 ATTRIBUTES

OF GOD

FROM

A TO Z

We have now come to the part of the book in which we'll examine attributes, or descriptions of God with all the letters of the alphabet!

You will usually find several words beginning with a given letter—see how many your family members can come up with.

After the suggested words, the one in bold will be the focus of the devotional. A story to illustrate the concept, questions to elicit discussion, and a sample prayer will enrich your time together.

Do you know any characteristics of God that start with the letter A?
Be sure everyone is speaking about God with reverence and respect. Here are some ideas for you.

ABBA	AMEN
ABSOLUTE	ANSWERING
ACTIVE	APT
ADVOCATE	ARTIST
AFFECTIONATE	ATTRACTIVE
ALMIGHTY	AUTHENTIC
ALPHA	AUTHOR
AMAZING	AUTHORITATIVE

Abba

The Almighty has a fatherly heart.

There's a story about a soldier during the Civil War in the United States who urgently needed to meet the president because of some tragedy in his family. He left the service and came to the White House, but he wasn't allowed to see the president! He went to a park and sat on a bench there, quite frustrated. A young man was passing by, and he wondered why the soldier was so upset. The soldier explained the dilemma. The young man suggested that the soldier follow him, and he led him through all levels of security to the president's parlor. The soldier still didn't understand who this young man was.

ASK

Why do you think the guards let the young man through?

When the young man looked into the president's office, the soldier heard Abraham Lincoln's voice: "What did you want, Todd?"

The young man replied, "Dad, this soldier wants to tell you something. Can you give him some time?" And the soldier was granted the president's time.

Thanks to the president's son Todd, a simple soldier got the hearing of the chief executive of the nation! Through the sacrifice of Jesus Christ, you and I have a right to enter the "parlor" of the almighty God and call Him "Father." Within a family, a father can be addressed in a variety of ways. In the Slavic culture a father can be addressed not only by name, but by many respectful titles: "husband," "Dad," "Daddy." Do you know what children in European Georgia call their fathers?

They call them the word for "mama"! Bulgarians call their fathers "bascha." And in Turkey they say "baba."

ASK

Do you know what Aramaic-speaking children in the time of Christ called their fathers?

They called their fathers "Abba." This word can be translated as "Father," or "Dad." We too can address God using this word. As Paul explains:

> Because we are his children, God has sent the Spirit of his Son
> into our hearts, prompting us to call out, "Abba, Father."
> **—GALATIANS 4:6** NLT

The Holy Spirit indwelling us inspires us to call to the Creator of the whole universe in this very way! In the days when the apostle Paul wrote these words, slaves and captives were not allowed to address the head of the household as "Abba." This special word was reserved only for sons and daughters.

There's another interesting feature of the word "Abba." We can address God with this word when we are in trouble. This is what Jesus did in a difficult moment of His life:

> He said, "Abba, Father, all things are possible for you. Remove
> this cup from me. Yet not what I will, but what you will."
> **—MARK 14:36**

Following Christ's example, we, too, have this secure way to call to God, "Abba! Father, help!" "Abba! Father"—the fatherly heart of God is revealed in these words.

PRAYER | **While you worship God, meditate on His fatherly heart. Thank Him for His openness and availability through Jesus Christ.**

BEAUTIFUL
BEGINNING
BELOVED
BEST
BESTOWER
BLESSED
BRAVE
BRIGHT
BRILLIANT

Do you know any characteristics of God that start with the letter B? Be sure everyone is speaking about God with reverence and respect. Here are some ideas for you.

Bright

In the bright light of God our sinfulness is seen clearly.

Anne Graham Lotz, the daughter of the late world-renowned evangelist Billy Graham, shared a story from her childhood. Her father often appeared on television, and usually the recordings took place at TV studios. But on one occasion it was arranged to record an interview at the Grahams' house. It was a very important event, as that interview was going to be watched by millions.

Anne and her mother cleaned the whole house. They took away all unnecessary items from the room, and rearranged the furniture in such a way that it would look nice on camera. The most effort was given to cleaning the carpet and dusting the furniture. They carefully wiped it all. It took them almost a whole day, and the room seemed to be ready for the shooting. A few hours before the interview had to be recorded, the TV crew came. They set up their equipment and placed big spotlights around the room. Cameras and microphones were all set. The lighting man turned on the lights, and Anne Graham saw the room anew—and was she embarrassed!

ASK

What do you think happened?

The bright light revealed dusty and previously unnoticed spots on the cabinet and the shelves. In the blindingly bright light, the room no longer seemed that clean. Anne and her mother didn't like seeing it. Later Anne shared that throughout the whole interview they felt uncomfortable because of the revealed filth. This example is a good illustration of one's relationship with God. In the Bible, God is revealed as Light:

> This is the message we have heard from him and proclaim to
> you, that God is light, and in him is no darkness at all.
> —1 JOHN 1:5

There are spots even on the bright sun, but "in Him there is no darkness." There are no spots in Him! The apostle John gives us an image of bright light in order to describe the absolute holiness of God. Before a person comes into contact with God, they live in darkness. They live not even noticing their sins. They live like everyone else, and sin like everyone else. Their conscience convicts them from time to time, but all in all, their efforts to fix their sin look like trying to clean a dark room. When a person accepts Christ into their heart by faith, the bright light of God shines inside and reveals all the sins! A person feels ashamed, and often tears of repentance run down the cheeks of a penitent sinner.

But this is what is interesting about the light of God: it does not illuminate the person's life just once, but it grows brighter and brighter in the Christian as time goes by. It is as if the lighting crew were cranking their spotlights' brightness up all the time. In such increasing light, dust will become visible even under the cabinets and in secret corners behind the couch! But how bright can this light be? In his letter to Timothy, Paul calls this bright light of God "inaccessible" for mankind:

He alone can never die, and he lives in light so brilliant that no
human can approach him. No human eye has ever seen him,
nor ever will. All honor and power to him forever! Amen.
—1 TIMOTHY 6:16 NLT

Inaccessible bright light—and we are not talking about spotlights. Perhaps
a blinding electric welding arc is a more suitable example. People can't look
at such light without protective glasses, or they would burn their eyes and go
blind. God's light in a person is not lit all at once, but gradually. Therefore, the
Christian life is said to be a "process of sanctification," i.e., the person is set apart
more and more for God, getting rid of his or her sins. Solomon says that the life
of the righteous is like the dawn:

The path of the righteous is like the light of dawn, which shines
brighter and brighter until full day.
—PROVERBS 4:18

As we grow in our friendship with God and draw closer to Him, His light
grows brighter in us. More and more sins that we should get rid of are revealed
to us. This will happen to us until the time when we at last stand face to face with
Him in eternity.

PRAYER | **While you worship God, meditate on the bright light of His holiness. Thank Him for Jesus Christ who has become our "protective glasses," and for His light that grows brighter and brighter.**

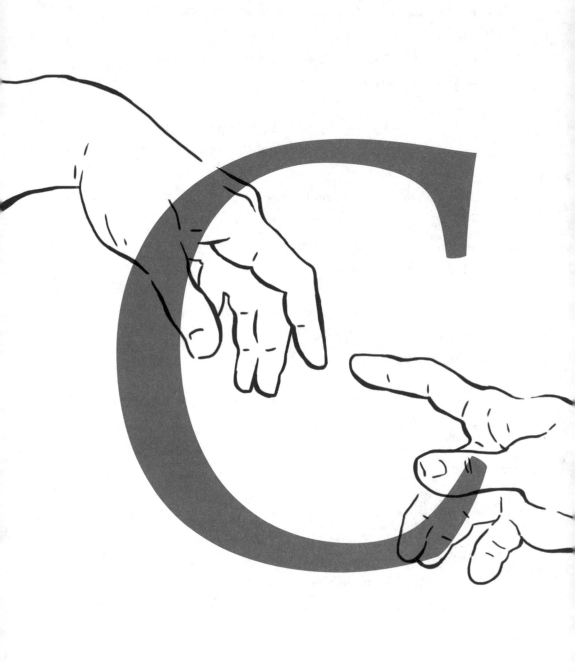

Do you know any characteristics of God that start with the letter C? Be sure everyone is speaking about God with reverence and respect. Here are some ideas for you.

CARING	COMMANDER
CAUSE	COMPANION
CHERISHED	CONSIDERATE
CHRIST	CORNERSTONE
CLEANSING	COUNSELOR
CLOSE	COURAGEOUS
COMFORTER	COVENANT
COMING	CREATIVE

Close

We never have to wonder if God is close—He is.

This is a story that tells God is always a prayer away. Here's how it goes: Once there was a man who had a dream. In the dream, three women came to a church to pray. Each had their problems and stresses that they brought to God. Each one of them prayed sincerely from the bottom of her heart, and each had tears running down her cheeks.

In answer to their prayers, Christ appeared to each one of them in this dream. He came to the first woman and wiped her tears, and then He leaned down and whispered something in her ear. This helped to distract from her problem and switch her attention to the Lord. Then the Savior put His arm around her shoulder and spoke with her softly for a long time. The woman's sad face started to transform gradually. With her face lifted up to the sky, she became more and more confident. It was obvious that the presence of Christ encouraged her and filled her with hope.

Jesus behaved differently with the second woman. He didn't tell her anything; He simply placed His arm on her shoulder and intensely looked in her eyes with God's love. After that intense look, the woman noticeably gained confidence and was no longer worried as she had been when she had first started to pray.

Christ didn't even approach the third woman. He just stood near, and then left her.

ASK

If you witnessed that situation, what would you have thought about the answers of the Lord? Why did He spend so much time with the first woman, and so little with the third?

Does it seem like the first woman had a very good relationship with Him, and the third was the most sinful of the three? This was exactly the way the man who had the dream interpreted it. But it turned out to be a misunderstanding!

An angel appeared to him and said, "You have misinterpreted your dream." The angel continued to explain. "The first woman was the furthest from God. Her faith was very weak, and that is why He had to spend so much time comforting and encouraging her. The second woman's faith was a bit stronger, and it took only a small encouragement from Christ to help her. But what about the third? The third woman knows Christ closely, and He knows her. They have experienced many wonderful moments together. Her faith in God is strong, and that is why she didn't need any special comfort from Him because she completely trusts Him!"

This story is based on a poem originally written in Russian by a woman named Lubov Vasenina. You probably guessed it is not a true story, but a parable, a made-up story to tell us about a spiritual truth. This story helps us think about God's closeness, which is not measured by our feelings, but rather by our trust in Him. God's deeper comforts go to those Christians who need them the most. This is also how parents treat their children. If a child is sick, he or she will get more attention. This principle is recorded in the New Testament:

On the contrary, the parts of the body that seem to be weaker are indispensable, and on those parts of the body that we think less honorable we bestow the greater honor, and our unpresentable parts are treated with greater modesty.
—1 CORINTHIANS 12:22–23

This God who teaches us to take care of the weak, doesn't He Himself behave the same way with us? Let us not assess God's proximity by our feelings. The Bible has more to say about God's closeness:

"For what great nation is there that has a god so near to it as the LORD our God is to us, whenever we call upon him?"
—DEUTERONOMY 4:7

God is near; He's at hand anytime His children call on Him in their sincere prayers.

PRAYER | **While you worship God, meditate on His daily nearness. Thank Him for always being near to His children—even at times when we don't feel it.**

Do you know any characteristics
of God that start with the letter D?
Be sure everyone is speaking
about God with reverence and
respect. Here are some ideas
for you.

DEFENDER
DELIVERER
DESIGNER
DETERMINED
DILIGENT
DOCTOR

Defender

In Jesus Christ you have a safe protection from evil.

Here is a story about a traveler who was walking through a forest in South America.[12]

He grew tired and sat down on a slanted tree to rest. When he sat, he heard an alarmed chirping sound coming from a bird. The traveler got up and moved closer to the tree where, above it, he saw two birds circling it. There on the tree he spotted chicks in a little nest. But he also saw a venomous snake crawling toward the tree. Its tongue flickered back and forth, and its eyes were fixed on the nest. Suddenly, the male bird disappeared, and the female, closely watching the viper, covered the chicks with her wings. After a short time the father bird returned with a green branch in his beak. He covered the female with it, and then flew up and sat on a higher branch of the same tree.

The snake had crept even closer, closer . . . and now was heading up the tree trunk. Closing in on the nest, it was about to strike when suddenly, as if having been struck itself, it lowered its head and slithered quickly down the tree! Then it hid in the tall grass.

ASK

Why do you think the snake didn't do the chicks any harm?

The traveler became very curious about the incident. He climbed up the tree and very carefully took the branch that the father bird had used to cover the mother bird and showed it to the locals. He learned that the branch the male bird used to defend the mother bird was from a bush that is poisonous to snakes. A small, helpless bird wisely used it as a safeguard!

Like that branch, Jesus is our safeguard before the forces of darkness. Day and night, He protects us from the harm that Satan, the evil serpent, wants to inflict on us. We cannot deal with that harm on our own, but together with Jesus our defender we can!

Harm and evil can take various forms. Satan wants to harm a person through fear, sadness, problems between friends, betrayal, loss of property, death of a loved one, or any manner of things that happen in life.

ASK

What are some other forms of harm and evil you can think of?

Harm and evil are always around this fallen world and will touch every person in some way or another. But the Bible says that under the Lord's protection we can find deliverance from all evil:

> The LORD will keep you from all evil;
>   he will keep your life.
> —PSALM 121:7

How does the Lord protect us? One way is through His commandments. God's ways are never to harm us, and His ways are not made up for no reason. God's ways are always best, and His rules are to protect us. He also defends us by helping us find a way out when temptation is strong. He will defend us against the devil's temptations.

The temptations in your life are no different from what others experience. And God is faithful. He will not allow the temptation to be more than you can stand. When you are tempted, he will show you a way out so that you can endure.

—1 CORINTHIANS 10:13 NLT

PRAYER | **Worship God who defends us. Thank Him for all the occasions in your life when you clearly saw His deliverance from evil, and also for the ones that you were never even aware of.**

*Do you know any characteristics
of God that start with the letter E?*
Be sure everyone is speaking
about God with reverence and
respect. Here are some ideas
for you.

EAGLE
ELOHIM
ETERNAL
EVANGELIST
EXAMPLE
EXPERT
EXTRAORDINARY

Eagle

Under God's wings is the safest place for you.

Many times in the Bible, we find words or ideas that stand for something. For example, when Jesus said, "I am the door" (John 10:9), He didn't literally mean He was made of wood or steel and came with a doorknob. In John 15:5, Jesus compares Himself to a vine and His followers to branches. These word pictures help us understand more about Him. We call these word pictures symbols.

The Bible uses the eagle as a symbol. Did you know that the eagle is mentioned in the Bible about thirty-four times? There are more than sixty types of eagles, and they are found all over the world, in every continent except Antarctica. This magnificent bird is admired for its size and power, and is often used as a symbol of freedom and strength.

The eagle has astonishing eyesight, keen enough to see up to two miles away, which helps it find prey, and its eyesight is four to five times better than that of humans. The eyes of an eagle take up about half its head size. An eagle can also see more colors than human beings can—another God-given ability that helps it hunt. Perhaps these traits led to the expression "eagle-eyed."

The beak of this "king of birds" is made of keratin, the same substance as your fingernails, and like nails, it is always growing.

Have you ever caught sight of a hummingbird? This tiny bird flutters, and its wings flap up to eighty times per second! And have you seen geese flying? They fly together in flocks, often in a V-formation.

In contrast, eagles fly alone. They do not flutter like a hummingbird—they soar. An eagle's nest is called an aerie, and can be over eight feet wide and up to thirteen feet deep. It is typically built at a higher elevation that those of other birds. This location gives the eagle the advantage of protection, and also serves as sort of a launching pad. Eagles pick up wind thermals, which are bubbles of air that rise from the ground in a column. God has designed the eagle with an interesting wing structure. They can soar for hours by catching wind currents, needing to flap their huge wings only periodically. And did you know that each wing has more than 1,250 feathers?[13] Imagine soaring high in the sky like an eagle!

Let's compare the eagle to some other birds. Canaries, for example, are pleasing little birds, but we mostly think of them inside a cage, singing. We can be like the canary when we'd rather stay safe in a cage, too timid to venture out and try new things. Or take the buzzard. You might see these birds squawking at the side of the road, eating up the carcass of a dead rodent. We too can act like buzzards when we squawk and complain, criticizing when we could be soaring above all that. Or consider the peacock, one of God's loveliest creations. Have you seen how it can spread its feathers and show off its colorful plumage? A person who struts around showing off, vain and self-focused, can behave like a peacock.[14]

ASK

How have you seen someone behave like a canary, a buzzard, a peacock, or an eagle? Which would you prefer to imitate?

Most people, given those choices, would choose the eagle. But here's something to consider: how many of us really want to be different than others? Author Mary Whelchel says, "If we want to soar like eagles, we must first accept the fact that eagles are different from other birds, and we'll have to be willing to be different, too. You can't soar with ordinary wings. It takes extraordinary and unique wings, such as eagles have."[15]

Do you remember Jesus' words? He prayed for His disciples, who were in the world but not of the world (John 17:14–16). In a way, an eagle, high above the rest, is in the world but above it. For we who are God's children, we are also in the world—we live on earth, we eat and play and work in the world—but our values are above the world's values. Our standards and our behavior must take their cue from God's ways, not from the culture around us. As the eagle flies alone, sometimes we might have to fly alone, taking a stand apart from the flock who follow the ways of the world. The Lord wants us to fly high like the eagle.

ASK

When is it hard to want to soar above the ways of the world?

An eagle's wings serve as a symbol of God's strength and His care for us: "You yourselves have seen . . . how I bore you on eagles' wings and brought you to myself" (Ex. 19:4). And we ourselves will soar high like an eagle when we are strengthened and refreshed by God:

> Those who trust in the LORD will find new strength.
> They will soar high on wings like eagles.
> They will run and not grow weary.
> They will walk and not faint.
> —ISAIAH 40:31 NLT

As Moses was saying farewell to the Israelites, he compared God to an eagle:

> "He encircled him, he cared for him,
> he kept him as the apple of his eye.
> Like an eagle that stirs up its nest,
> that flutters over its young,

spreading out its wings, catching them,
    bearing them on its pinions,
the LORD alone guided him."
—DEUTERONOMY 32:10–12

In this passage above, Moses adds something else to his comparison of God to an eagle: gentleness. Does this surprise you?

ASK

Why or why not?

The eagle is a majestic part of God's creation. The eagle is strong yet gentle, like God. The eagle sits high above, protected in its aerie yet ready to launch out and soar. Like the eagle, God gives His children the ability to soar, resting on the wind currents without worry, without flapping our wings repeatedly. When we have been born into God's family, He who strengthens the eagle also strengthens us when we call on Him.

PRAYER | **Worship the Lord who protects us. Thank Him for His secure protection and patience. Ask Him to help you soar!**

ASK
───────

Do you know any characteristics of God that start with the letter F? Be sure everyone is speaking about God with reverence and respect. Here are some ideas for you.

FAITHFUL
FARMER
FATHER
FIRM
FIRST
FORMIDABLE
FORTRESS
FOUNDER
FREE
FRIEND

First

Give God the first, and He will take care of the rest.

There was a brother and sister who lived in Ukraine, a large country in eastern Europe. Their names were Bogdan and Olya. Bogdan was twelve and Olya was eleven. One day they decided to prepare the dinner and give their mom a break.

"Sit here on the couch," Olya told her, "and relax with your book. Bogdan and I will make supper tonight." So Mother made herself comfortable in the living room while the kids were busy in the kitchen.

They had looked for recipes online and found one for borscht, a popular Ukrainian soup. Borscht is a delicious meal with an inviting aroma, the recipe promised. "Try our recipe and you'll have a steaming, hearty, delicious, and nourishing meal. Perfect for a chilly, winter day. And excellent served cold, too!" The recipe called for potatoes, meat, water, carrots, beans, beets, onions, and cabbage. Bogdan and Olya studied the photos of the finished product and saw that borscht is red.

ASK
───────

What do you think gives borscht its red color?

Bogdan and Olya found all the ingredients in the kitchen and laid them on the counter. Bogdan pulled out the large stew pot and set it on the stove. He carefully turned on the burner beneath it.

The children chatted and laughed as they prepared the ingredients, peeling the potatoes and carrots, and washing the beans. With a thudding plonk, the potatoes went into the pot. Olya added beans. Bogdan put in carrots. The pot was warming up. How delicious the meal would be, and how happy Mother would feel! In went cabbage, meat, beets, and the onions, which made their eyes sting. But they didn't mind. They couldn't wait to serve Mother the borscht. Bogdan sprinkled in salt and Olya added a dash of pepper. Soon the house would be filled with the delicious aroma of simmering borscht, tickling Mother's senses as she read her book. But wait—what was that stinky, scorching smell?

Oh no! Water! They had forgotten the water! "Hurry, Bogdan," hissed Olya. "We forgot the water!"

Quick as a wink, Bogdan poured water into the pot. *ttsssssssshhhsssh* . . . they heard an unwelcome sizzle from the concoction. All the ingredients were in the pot, but instead of the borscht described in the recipe, they had a sodden mess. What went wrong?

Though they had all the right ingredients, they had put them into the pot in the wrong order. It was important to put everything into the pot in a certain order: water first, followed by the meat and potatoes, then the rest.

Something similar often happens in our lives, too. Everyone wants to live happily, and we look for our own recipe for happiness. People fill up the "pots" of their lives with all kinds of "ingredients"—such as a nice car, popular friends, the most updated cellphone.

ASK

What other "ingredients" do we put in the "pots" of our lives to find happiness?

Some people will even toss "going to church" into their pots, but they still do not find true happiness. A happy life must come from following the right order.

We find the correct order in the Bible: God must come first. God is our Creator, and deserves to take first place in our lives. If we put Him first, other things will fall into their right order. Jesus Himself said,

> "Seek first the kingdom of God and his righteousness, and all
> these things will be added to you."
> —MATTHEW 6:33

We can count on God: if we put Him first, He'll take care of all the rest!

Bogdan and Olya's mother was very understanding about the mess, and the next day they tried again—this time putting the ingredients in the right order, and cooking a delectable meal.

PRAYER | **Worship God, who is always first in the universe. Thank Him for promising to take care of everything in our lives.**

ASK

*Do you know any characteristics
of God that start with the letter G?*
Be sure everyone is speaking
about God with reverence and
respect. Here are some ideas
for you.

Generous

God shows you His generosity without any strings attached.

There are many stories about the generosity of Alexander the Great, a renowned commander of ancient Greece. On one occasion, he announced he would pay off all the debts of his soldiers. But his soldiers looked on his decision with suspicion rather than with appreciation. Apparently, even so long ago, people knew the saying, "There's no such thing as a free lunch."

The ancient Greek historian Arrian described what happened. Many of Alexander's soldiers were getting married or had already gotten married. He had all the Macedonian (Greek) men who had married Asian women register their names. It turned out there were more than ten thousand such marriages! And Alexander gave them all a wedding gift.

He also used the opportunity to pay off the debts his soldiers owed. Arrian explains, "At first, only a few registered their names, as the soldiers feared that this was a test—a way for Alexander to discover which of his men were not getting by on their pay and which were living extravagantly."[16] But Alexander reprimanded the men for not trusting him. He assured them that as their leader, they could trust his word. So he set up tables in the camp. He put money on the tables. He told his assistants to pay off the debt of any man who came with his debts written on a paper, but to *not* take down his name.

Now the soldiers believed Alexander! They knew he was showing his generosity, not trying to trick them. Paying off the money the soldiers owed came to about twenty thousand talents, a huge amount of money.

ASK

What do you think about this act of Alexander the Great?

At first glance, it's a very generous act! But historians are skeptical of the idea that Alexander was acting from a good heart with pure motives. Perhaps by this act, the great commander wanted to buy the loyalty of his soldiers.

Sometimes our friends remind us, "Help me out. I have helped you before, and you owe me one!" A person's generosity is often tainted with an expectation for some gain. We are well aware of the "generosity" of politicians who start to act (repairing highways, for example) right before the elections, thereby trying to buy votes and win. In one Chicago neighborhood shortly before an election, residents were treated to sturdy new garbage cans by a candidate running for alderman on the city council. A coincidence? This is not generosity at all, but rather insidiously disguised greed!

ASK

Can you think of an example of someone doing something that looked generous but was really done with selfish motives? Now think of a time someone was generous with a pure heart.

God's generosity is completely different from that of man. God gives from His perfect nature. He does not give generously with a hidden motive. Think about Jesus' generosity. On one occasion He fed a crowd of five thousand hungry people, and at the same time He gave them more bread than they needed.

They all ate and were satisfied. And they took up twelve baskets
full of broken pieces [of bread] and of the fish.

—MARK 6:42–43

Did Jesus know how much the crowd needed? Of course, He did. Could He
have multiplied the bread to provide exactly as much as needed and not a bite
more? Yes. By His action, Jesus wasn't bribing people (as Alexander the Great
likely did with his soldiers). Not only was Jesus providing for the needs of the
people in that place and at the time, but it gave Him great joy to do so. And that
should be true of us, if we follow His example.

PRAYER	Worship God who generously provides us with everything we need. Think of the things that you as a family could give away to others, and thank God for being able to minister to other people.

HAPPY
HEALER
HEAVENLY
HELPER
HERITAGE
HERO
HOLISTIC
HOLY
HONEST
HUMBLE
HUSBAND

*Do you know any characteristics
of God that start with the letter H?*
Be sure everyone is speaking
about God with reverence and
respect. Here are some ideas
for you.

Holy

Our sinfulness is clearly seen when compared with His holiness.

There is an old story about a rich man visiting the town of Gaza when he overheard two monks talking. Brother John was saying, "The more I understand my own sinfulness, the closer I feel to God."

Brother George answered, "Yes, I get it. I feel the same way!"

The rich man listening approached the two men. "That doesn't make sense to me. The more sinful you feel, the closer you get to God?"

"Yes," the two monks chorused.

"Can you explain that to me?"

Both monks studied the man. He was wearing a tailored suit made of high quality fabric. His comfortable shoes had no holes and were cut from the finest leather. He carried a fancy case for his important papers, and he carried himself proudly. In contrast, each monk was wearing a simple robe and a pair of ordinary sandals.

Brother John said, "Please tell me. When you're at home in your own town, how do you describe yourself?"

The rich man said, "I'm an important citizen there. Everyone knows me. People want to shake my hand."

The monks nodded. Then Brother George asked, "If you went to the city of Caesarea, how would you describe yourself?"

The rich man thought. "Well, not very important, actually."

Brother John said, "And if you went to the very large and noble city of Antioch?"

"I have to say I'd feel like anyone else there—a common person, just like most anyone else."

So Brother George said, "Now imagine going to the great, world-famous city of Constantinople. And that you've been granted an audience with the emperor himself! How do you feel about yourself then?"

ASK

How do you think the rich man will answer this time?

The story goes on. This time the rich man said, "Oh, that's easy. The emperor would be in fine clothes sitting on a throne inside his majestic palace. Next to him, I'd look like . . . well, I'd look like a beggar."

"And," added Brother John, "even if we put on a fancy robe and went near the emperor, we'd still be a simple person inside."

"And that's how it is when a person approaches God," Brother George told him kindly. "Next to Him, the perfect holy God, we know we're sinners. And the closer we draw near to Him, the more we realize He is holy and we are not."

"Do you understand better now?" Brother John asked the rich man.

"Yes," the rich man assured his new friends. "Thank you for explaining this to me. Your story makes me love God more, when I think of how He *wants* us to draw near to Him!"

Peter in the Bible had a similar reaction when Jesus miraculously caused Peter and his friends to catch a boatload of fish after they had been fishing all night with nothing to show for it.

When Simon Peter realized what had happened, he fell to his knees before Jesus and said, "Oh, Lord, please leave me—I'm such a sinful man."

—LUKE 5:8 NLT

Next to the Son of God, Peter clearly saw himself as a sinner. In the blinding spotlight of God's holiness, Peter felt that he was a "black spot"! It is always like this. The ones who love sinning are repelled by this holiness, but for the ones willing to repent and change, that is what draws them nearer and reveals their sins. If you say that you are growing spiritually but at the same time you don't see more sins revealed in your life, then you are not coming closer to God but are rather stagnant.

PRAYER | **Worship the holy God, in whose light we see our sins. Thank God for Jesus Christ, who came to this earth and died on the cross to give us forgiveness and cleanse us from our sins.**

ASK

Do you know any characteristics of God that start with the letter I?
Be sure everyone is speaking about God with reverence and respect. Here are some ideas for you.

IMMANENT
IMMANUEL
IMMORTAL
INCOMPREHENSIBLE
INEXPRESSIBLE
INGENIOUS
INSIGHTFUL
INSISTENT
INTERCESSOR

Inexpressible

Our language is so meager and incapable of describing the riches of our Maker.

Here is an often-retold story from India. Six people who were standing around reached out to touch something in front of them, but the people were all blind and therefore could not see what they were touching. So they described what they felt. The first person said, "I feel something large and hard. It is a wall!" The second blind person answered, "No, it's round and long. It's a snake!" The third person said, "It is pointed and sharp. We're touching a spear!" The fourth blind person said, "It is very tall and thick—it must be a tree!" The fifth objected: "It is wide and thin—surely it's a fan to hold in your hand." The sixth said: "No, it's a rope. It's long and thin."

ASK

What do you think these blind people were touching? They were touching an elephant!

Maybe you have guessed that the first blind person touched the elephant's side. The second one was touching his trunk. The third touched the elephant's tusks. The fourth touched the elephant's leg. The fifth touched the elephant's ear. The sixth touched the tail. A snake, a wall, a spear, a tree, a fan, a rope: all of these were only parts of the picture, but each blind person failed to describe anything that would have resembled an elephant.

The same happens to our knowledge of God. When we see a criminal sentenced to prison, we say, "God is just!" When we see an orphan adopted, we say, "God is merciful."

And when we come across biblical verses about God, we come up with various ideas about Him. Just like the blind men in the parable, we "feel" God with our thoughts and emotions, and try to describe Him. And God lets us do that! He reveals Himself gradually because no one can comprehend God in His entirety.

We cannot comprehend God's mind: "The LORD is the everlasting God, the Creator of the ends of the earth. He does not faint or grow weary; his understanding is unsearchable" (Isa. 40:28).

We cannot understand God's thoughts. He tells us: "For as the heavens are higher than the earth, so are my ways higher than your ways and my thoughts than your thoughts" (Isa. 55:9).

We cannot fathom God's deeds. Even the wisest person ever, Solomon, said: "I realized that no one can discover everything God is doing under the sun. Not even the wisest people discover everything, no matter what they claim" (Eccl. 8:17 NLT).

Novatian, a priest in the early church, also pondered about our inability to express God with words:

> We pass beyond our power of fit conception, nor can human eloquence put forth a power commensurate with His greatness. ... He is greater than all language, and no statement can express Him. Indeed, if any statement could express Him, He would be less than human speech which could by such statement comprehend and gather up all that He is. All our thoughts about

Him will be less than He, and our loftiest utterances will be trivialities in comparison with Him.[17]

Here is a way to illustrate this story in your family devotions time. Let two participants sit across from each other (it can be you and your spouse). The children should close their eyes. And then, when they can't see it, take a dollar bill and look at it from your side, and your wife should look from hers. Take turns naming out loud the details you see on the money, one at a time. The children's task is to guess what object is being described. What makes it difficult is the fact that the front and the back of the banknote are different. For example, one person might say, "I see a building" but another might say, "No, there's no building; but I see the portrait of a man!" Do this until the children guess that you are describing a piece of money. Then you can draw a conclusion that even eternity will not be enough to comprehend God entirely; we will only understand some part of Him!

PRAYER | Suggest worshiping God not out loud, but rather in the quietness of your hearts. Sometimes silence is the best way to tell God, "You are so great that we run out of words to express it!" Take enough time to pray in silence, and close this time with "Amen."

*Do you know any characteristics
of God that start with the letter J?*
Be sure everyone is speaking
about God with reverence and
respect. Here are some ideas
for you.

JEW
  (ABOUT CHRIST)
JEWEL
JEWELER
JOYFUL
JUDGE

Jeweler

God uses trials to prepare you for eternity.

A man named Ryan who worked in a jewelry shop tells this story about the process of metal purification he tinkered with as a younger man (hopefully making sure to take proper safety precautions!). "We took lead plates and crumbled them into a spoon," he said. He went on, "Then we heated the spoon in fire and watched the crumbles turn into a silvery liquid. Usually there was a thin film of dirt particles and slag covering the reflective surface of the molten lead, and we carefully swept it away with a straw. This is called purifying—to purify is to take away anything impure. For a long time I thought that gold was purified in the same way. But that's not the case at all."

Ryan continued his story about how gold is purified. He explained, "Nowadays gold is purified of its impurities using chlorine vapors, but in ancient times another method was used. They used to melt gold in a special container made of porous clay. Porous means something that has tiny spaces for air or liquid to pass through. For example, a sponge or a cork is porous; so is your skin. Anyway, the container they used in ancient times was called a cupel. And that method of purification was called cupellation."

Ryan explained that gold from a goldmine is not pure; it contains flecks of copper, zinc, silver, and iron. That's why it must be purified. In ancient times, a jeweler would take raw gold and throw it into the cupel. Then pieces of lead, a small amount of salt, tin, and barley bran were added too. Then the jeweler sealed the crucible with clay and placed it into a furnace for five days.

Ryan finished his explanation. He said, "During the purification process, the lead would take all the impurities, which were then soaked into the porous walls of the container called the cupel. But the gold would not be absorbed. When the jeweler got the vessel back from the furnace and opened it, there was a sparkling ball of pure gold at the bottom!"

The Bible tells us that God is a Jeweler:

> "He will purify the sons of Levi and refine them like gold and
> silver, and they will bring offerings in righteousness to the LORD."
> —MALACHI 3:3

The faith of Israel was contaminated with impurities. The people sinned, and sometimes they even worshiped the false gods of the nations around them. So God, out of His love for them, began to purify their faith through trials. And today God is the same! With us He acts as a Jeweler by letting various trials enter our lives to purify our faith.

ASK

What are some trials we go through?

Peter describes the process like this:

> So be truly glad. There is wonderful joy ahead, even though
> you must endure many trials for a little while. These trials will
> show that your faith is genuine. It is being tested as fire tests and
> purifies gold—though your faith is far more precious than mere

gold. So when your faith remains strong through many trials, it will bring you much praise and glory and honor on the day when Jesus Christ is revealed to the whole world.

—1 PETER 1:6–7 NLT

ASK

How can trials or problems purify us? How can they make us stronger in our faith? How does allowing trials show us that God loves us?

God the Jeweler keeps everything under His control, and He permits these things to teach us to trust Him more. God desires our faith to be strong on the day when Jesus Christ is revealed. He wants it to be pure as gold so that we can get praise, glory, and honor!

PRAYER | Together, worship God the Jeweler, who purifies us through various trials and prepares us for the second coming of Jesus Christ.

Do you know any characteristics of God that start with the letter K? Be sure everyone is speaking about God with reverence and respect. Here are some ideas for you.

KEEPER
KIND
KING
KING OF KINGS
KNOWING

Keeper

Nothing can snatch us out of Jesus' hand!

One day Jenna was walking home from school, taking a different route than usual. She was humming to herself, enjoying the sunny day, and remembering that she had had a great day at school. Suddenly Jenna gasped as a huge, lion-colored dog appeared in front of the house she was passing. A low growl started in its throat. Jenna realized the animal was likely defending its territory and looked at her as a threat. The growl became more intense, and the dog began to bark menacingly.

ASK

How would you feel if you were in Jenna's place? What do you think she should do?

Jenna was so afraid she could barely move. But she was able to croak, "Hello? Someone? Please call off your dog!"

"Lilac, back off! C'mon, girl!" Jenna whirled around when she heard the deep voice of the dog's owner. The dog also whirled around at the sound of her owner's voice and obediently followed him back into the house.

"Thank you!" Jenna said, and continued home.

ASK

What might have happened if Jenna had yelled at the dog or tried to outrun it?

Let us think about what had happened. Calling for the dog's owner was indeed the best solution. Why was that? Because Lilac knew her owner, the one who kept her and cared for her, and would not have listened to anyone else.

Jesus said the shepherd "calls his own sheep by name. . . . and they follow him because they know His voice" (John 10:3–4 NLT).

The situation with the dog resembles the world we live in. Satan wants nothing more than to do us harm; he is certainly not our keeper. But we can know the one who is. "The LORD is your keeper; the LORD is your shade on your right hand" (Ps. 121:5).

During His earthly ministry, Jesus commanded evil spirits with authority, and they obeyed Him. When a man who was plagued by an evil spirit shouted at Jesus to "go away," Jesus rebuked him and ordered him to leave the man.

> "Be silent and come out of him!" And when the demon had
> thrown him down in their midst, he came out of him, having
> done him no harm.
> —LUKE 4:35

We as humans would be powerless before Satan and his demonic army if we did not have God as our keeper. We can always call on Him in prayer, asking for His help. Think about this wonderful possibility made available to us—to turn to God in prayer!

PRAYER | **Worship the great God whose voice is obeyed by all creation, even including the devil and his demons. Thank Him for being our keeper.**

LAMB
LAST
LAWYER
LEADER
LIFE-GIVING
LIGHT
LIGHTHOUSE
LION

LIVING
LOGICAL
LONG-SUFFERING
LORD
LORD OF LORDS
LOVE
LOVING

Loving

One knows God and the other doesn't, but God loves them both.

The man was anxiously waiting for the doctor to come into the examination room to remove the stitches on his thumb. When the doctor finally entered, he noticed that his patient, a gentleman of about eighty years old, was obviously in a hurry to get going.

"Do you have someplace you need to be?" the doctor asked, half joking. Where, he wondered, could this senior citizen possibly need to go that was so urgent?

The older man's voice trembled as he admitted he had an appointment to make, soon, by nine in the morning. The doctor efficiently removed the stitches and tended to the wound. While he was working, the doctor could not resist asking,

"It must be awfully important since you're in such a hurry."
"I need to make it on time to the hospital to feed my sick wife
her breakfast," the older man said.

Then the doctor asked what was wrong with her. The elderly man answered that she had been diagnosed with Alzheimer's disease. The doctor glanced at his watch and asked whether the man's wife would worry if he was slightly late. To the doctor's utter surprise, the man said that his wife, alas, hadn't recognized him for the last five years.

"She doesn't even know who I am to her," the man added, shaking his head. The doctor exclaimed in amazement, "And you still go there every morning despite the fact that she doesn't even know who you are?"

The man smiled kindly at the doctor and replied, "She doesn't know who I am, but I know who she is."[18]

ASK

What did this man mean when he said, "She doesn't know who I am, but I know who she is"?

With these words, the man expressed his selfless love for his wife. She was not able to give anything back to him, but he loved and cared for her without any gain for himself. This is what God calls Himself in the Bible—He is Love itself:

> Anyone who does not love does not know God, because God is love.
> **—1 JOHN 4:8**

The words "God is love" reveal the whole character of God to us. God's love always seeks the good of others and not of Himself. It explains why Jesus Christ died on the cross for our sins. He suffered to make us prosper.

Like the man from this story, the Lord God continues to love and care for all people on the earth. They are His beloved. He loves even those who do not know Him. We need to follow God's example and love every person we come across along our life's path. We are also called to tell them about the selfless love of God.

ASK

If you could give one characteristic of yourself, what would it be?

The Bible describes God in numerous ways, as we've already discovered in our worship times together.

ASK

What does it mean to you that the Bible comes out and says, "God is love"? In what ways does He show His love?

PRAYER | **Worship God while thinking of His selfless love. Thank Him for having loved you long ago, for still loving you, and for His willingness to love you always.**

MAGNANIMOUS
MAN
  (JESUS CHRIST)
MASTER
MENTOR
MERCIFUL
MESSIAH

MIGHTY
MIRACLE WORKER
MISSIONARY
MONARCH
MULTIFACETED
MYSTERY

Missionary

Christ came to enemies as a friend.

In 1956 a group of American missionaries left for Ecuador to preach the good news to a South American tribe called Auca (which means "savages"). The tribe was very violent, and they were known to immediately kill any white people who tried to approach their territory. Nate Saint was part of the group. The missionaries tried to establish contact with the tribe. At first, they would fly over in an airplane and lower baskets with food, and later the missionaries even managed to get the tribe to eat hamburgers and drink lemonade together with them. Everything seemed to progress quite well until one Sunday, on January 8, 1956, when someone from a helicopter spotted the bodies of five white men on the riverbank. It was clear that they were missionaries who had been attacked and killed.

The missionaries had rifles with them, so they could have saved their own lives, but they decided not to. Nate Saint, along with the other four, was killed with a spear. Pages from the New Testament were scattered around him. His life was over. Back home he was survived by his wife, Marj, and their little son, Steve.

ASK

What do you think happened next?

The missionaries' death could have been the end of the story, but for God it was just the beginning. Years later, other missionaries came again. They translated the New Testament into the tribe's language, and many Auca savages accepted Christ. Mincaye, the man who killed the missionary Nate Saint, also repented of his sins and became a follower of Christ.

ASK

What do you think happened after that?

It wasn't easy for Steve to forgive his father's murderer. It was also difficult for him to accept Mincaye as his brother in Christ, but through the power of God's love he did. And later it was Mincaye who baptized Steve according to his faith in Jesus Christ, and he became his spiritual mentor. Their relationship became so intimate and deep that Steve's children call him lovingly "Grandpa Mincaye." A photo of Steve Saint together with the Auca savage, who was a murderer but was redeemed by the blood of Christ, is quite famous in missionary circles! They embrace each other as brothers. Mincaye remained faithful the rest of his life, and when he died in April 2020, Nate's son Steve wrote an obituary for the man who had killed his father.[19]

ASK

Does anything surprise you about this story?

This story is a great reminder of what had happened two thousand years ago with the greatest Missionary, Jesus Christ. He came to humankind with the good news, but people, just like the Auca, treated him with hostility. He could have stood up for Himself, but He chose not to. And He was eventually put to death:

He came to his own people, and even they rejected him.
—JOHN 1:11 NLT

But His missionary spirit couldn't be stopped by death! Christ rose on the third day, and instead of revenge, He showed love to His enemies by sending His disciples into the world:

> "You will be my witnesses, telling people about me every-
> where—in Jerusalem, throughout Judea, in Samaria, and to the
> ends of the earth."
> —ACTS 1:8 NLT

This was the very call that once stirred Nate's heart and the hearts of his four missionary friends. It was this very call of Christ that prompted the descendants of the murdered missionaries to return to the violent savages. God still sends His missionaries even today. Will you answer His call?

ASK

Where can you be a missionary?

PRAYER | **Worship Christ, the Missionary who came to our hostile world. Thank God for the people who shared the good news with you, and for the ones you will tell about Christ this week.**

Do you know any characteristics of God that start with the letter N? Be sure everyone is speaking about God with reverence and respect. Here are some ideas for you.

NAVIGATOR
NEEDED
NEW
NICE
NOBLE

Navigator

One can see better from the top,
so trust the Lord with complete confidence.

The modern driver can hardly imagine traveling far without a navigation gadget. Nowadays the navigator is an app on the phone or in the car or on a device that easily fits in the palm of one's hand. It shows the driver the route to the desired destination.

ASK

Where can a navigator find instructions for the route?

In 1985, when the first navigator was invented, maps were recorded on tape cassettes. As the car moved, the cassettes needed to be changed, which was very inconvenient. By 1995, navigators were improved, thanks to the GPS, the positioning system that uses satellites. Since that time, the navigator "recognizes" its position by communicating with satellites orbiting the Earth high in space. This is why the car equipped with the navigator can seamlessly receive the signal wherever it is: high in the mountains, or on a flat field. It's only when the car moves through a tunnel or a dead zone where reception is blocked or when its battery is dead that the navigator doesn't work.

"One can see better from the top." These words apply not only to navigation devices, but to people. The all-seeing God from above shows people the right way, even when they think otherwise:

> "Yet the house of Israel says, 'The way of the Lord is not just.' O house of Israel, are my ways not just? Is it not your ways that are not just?"
> —EZEKIEL 18:29

ASK

When we can't see the whole way—the big picture—who should we trust? Why?

Jesus Christ calls Himself not a mere navigator; He claims to be the Living Way to the Father in heaven, saying:

> "I am the way, and the truth, and the life. No one comes to the Father except through me."
> —JOHN 14:6

Jesus ascended into heaven, but His teaching is recorded here in the Bible; therefore, anyone can measure their lives against God's ideas. In other words, the Bible can be called our navigator through life.

PRAYER | **Worship God, who constantly desires to lead you to the right path. Thank Him for leading us through the tunnels.**

ASK

*Do you know any characteristics
of God that start with the letter O?*
Be sure everyone is speaking
about God with reverence and
respect. Here are some ideas
for you.

OBJECTIVE
OBSERVANT
OMNIPOTENT
OMNIPRESENT
OMNISCIENT
ONE
ONLY
ONLY BEGOTTEN
　(ABOUT CHRIST)
ORIGINAL

Omnipotent, Omnipresent, Omniscient

*The attributes of God's supremacy are subject
to His love and wisdom.*

Today's selection is a little different in that we are going to talk about three attributes of God rather than one, but these three are related. We already know that we can imitate or desire to be like God in some of His characteristics: generous, loving, sacrificial, and others, though we'll never be perfectly any of these because we are not God. But today's characteristics belong to God and God alone: omnipotent, omnipresent, and omniscient.

The prefix "omni" means all. Everything. The whole enchilada.

Based on this, what do you think *omnipresent* means?

"Potent" means power. What does it mean to say "God is omnipotent"?

The letters "s-c-i-e-n-t" make us think of knowledge, or knowing. How is God omniscient?

There is a Bible story that will tell us about all three of these attributes of God. It is recorded in 2 Kings 6:8–23. It speaks about Elisha, the prophet of

God. It is important to understand that there was nothing miraculous about the prophet himself, and the reason for all the supernatural manifestations was God, with whom Elisha had a close relationship. We can have some fun with this by reading it out loud and everyone taking a turn (you might number the lines or paragraphs and assign each person his or her parts).

THE OMNISCIENCE OF GOD

The first episode, 2 Kings 6:8–12, shows that the omniscient God revealed to His prophet the innermost thoughts of the king of Syria. It is written out below in the New Living Translation but of course, you may use any version of the Bible you prefer.

> When the king of Aram was at war with Israel, he would confer with his officers and say, "We will mobilize our forces at such and such a place."
>
> But immediately Elisha, the man of God, would warn the king of Israel, "Do not go near that place, for the Arameans are planning to mobilize their troops there." So the king of Israel would send word to the place indicated by the man of God. Time and again Elisha warned the king, so that he would be on the alert there.
>
> The king of Aram became very upset over this. He called his officers together and demanded, "Which of you is the traitor? Who has been informing the king of Israel of my plans?"
>
> "It's not us, my lord the king," one of the officers replied. "Elisha, the prophet in Israel, tells the king of Israel even the words you speak in the privacy of your bedroom!"

ASK

What is going on in this scene? (The king of Aram is trying to plot against Israel, but the Israelites always seemed to find out his plans.) *Was Elisha omniscient? How did he know the plans of the king of Aram?*

THE OMNIPRESENCE OF GOD

In the second episode, 2 Kings 6:13–17, we read of a servant who didn't know what Elisha knew assuredly—that God is present with His people in every place.

> "Go and find out where he is," the king commanded, "so I can send troops to seize him."
>
> And the report came back: "Elisha is at Dothan." So one night the king of Aram sent a great army with many chariots and horses to surround the city.
>
> When the servant of the man of God [Elisha's servant] got up early the next morning and went outside, there were troops, horses, and chariots everywhere. "Oh, sir, what will we do now?" the young man cried to Elisha.
>
> "Don't be afraid!" Elisha told him. "For there are more on our side than on theirs!" Then Elisha prayed, "O LORD, open his eyes and let him see!" The LORD opened the young man's eyes, and when he looked up, he saw that the hillside around Elisha was filled with horses and chariots of fire. (NLT)

ASK

What does this scene tell us about God's omnipresence? What do we learn about God's care for Elisha's servant, a seemingly insignificant person in the story?

No matter how distant God's presence may seem, the Omnipresent is close to us and sends us His timely assistance and protection.

THE OMNIPOTENCE OF GOD

The third episode, 2 Kings 6:18–23, reveals to us the omnipotence of God when He "turns off" the sight of the Syrian army.

> As the Aramean army advanced toward him, Elisha prayed, "O LORD, please make them blind." So the LORD struck them with blindness as Elisha had asked.
>
> Then Elisha went out and told them, "You have come the wrong way! This isn't the right city! Follow me, and I will take you to the man you are looking for." And he led them to the city of Samaria.
>
> As soon as they had entered Samaria, Elisha prayed, "O LORD, now open their eyes and let them see." So the LORD opened their eyes, and they discovered that they were in the middle of Samaria.
>
> When the king of Israel saw them, he shouted to Elisha, "My father, should I kill them? Should I kill them?"
>
> "Of course not!" Elisha replied. "Do we kill prisoners of war? Give them food and drink and send them home again to their master."
>
> So the king made a great feast for them and then sent them home to their master. After that, the Aramean raiders stayed away from the land of Israel. (NLT)

So, all the laws of the universe, including the processes of the human body, are subject to God alone, and only He has authority over everything. Even today God is capable of doing anything that aligns with His good purposes.

What other conclusions can we draw from this story? The story closes with God's prophet Elisha not willing to destroy the enemies, but preferring to feed them. By this the Scripture highlights the fact that the attributes of God's supremacy—omniscience, omnipresence, and omnipotence—are subject to His love and wisdom.

God used hostile situations to teach His lessons to the servant of Elisha, to the Syrians, and to the king.

PRAYER | **Worship God while contemplating His omnipresence, omniscience, and omnipotence. Thank Him for the fact that all these attributes of His supremacy are subject to His love.**

PATIENT	POET
PEACE	PRECIOUS
PERFECT	PRIEST
PERFUMER	PRINCIPAL
PERSISTENT	PROSECUTOR
PERSON	PROVIDER
PERSONAL	PUNCTUAL
PHENOMENAL	PUNISHING
PHILANTHROPIST	PURPOSE
PHYSICIAN	PURPOSEFUL
PIERCED	

Perfumer

The fragrance of the gospel is pleasant to God.

ASK

What do you think a perfumer is? Right! A perfumer is someone who sells perfume or who prepares perfume or, more specifically, perfumery compositions.

Way back in 1760, James Henry Creed, who owned a small sewing shop, founded a company and called it the House of Creed. His company provided the royalty of his day with custom clothing and good-smelling leather gloves, as well as fragrances. In fact, in 1791, the king of England commissioned the House of Creed to create its first fragrance, fittingly called Royal English Leather.[20]

Since then, the family has remained involved in manufacturing expensive perfumery. From the start, they made perfumes for the royal families. And today, centuries later, James Creed's descendants make perfumes specifically for famous actors and politicians. It is strictly prohibited to counterfeit these exclusive fragrances. For example, in 2005, they created the fragrance Love in White that was unofficially nicknamed the Aroma of the White House, because it was the favorite of the First Lady of the United States.

ASK

In what way does each person want to feel unique, a little different from others?

Every person wants to highlight his or her uniqueness. This applies to their names, clothes, and even perfumes. Where did this human desire originate? It comes from God because we were created in the image and likeness of God.

We read in the Bible that the Lord is well versed in fragrances! As the Greatest Perfumer, He commanded His priests to make a special composition of fragrant substances, which were used to fill the tabernacle of the Lord with a special aroma:

> The LORD said to Moses, "Gather fragrant spices—resin drop-
> lets, mollusk shell, and galbanum—and mix these fragrant spices
> with pure frankincense, weighed out in equal amounts. Using the
> usual techniques of the incense maker, blend the spices together
> and sprinkle them with salt to produce a pure and holy incense.
> Grind some of the mixture into a very fine powder and put it in
> front of the Ark of the Covenant, where I will meet with you in
> the Tabernacle. You must treat this incense as most holy. Never
> use this formula to make this incense for yourselves. It is reserved
> for the LORD, and you must treat it as holy."
> —**EXODUS 30:34–37** NLT

If we lived at that time, then every time we came to a worship service, we would have smelled the exclusive fragrance made according to the recipe of the Almighty Himself!

ASK

Why do you think it was forbidden to use this recipe for a fragrance for any other purpose?

This special frankincense was used exclusively to emphasize God's holiness! Back then it was an important lesson for Israel. But does God still have a favorite fragrance? Think about this:

> But thanks be to God, who in Christ always leads us in trium-
> phal procession, and through us spreads the fragrance of the
> knowledge of him everywhere.
> —2 CORINTHIANS 2:14

ASK

What is God's favorite fragrance today? How can you and I spread the fragrance of knowing him? Words about God shared by us with our friends are the most desired fragrance to God today.

PRAYER | **Worship God who gave us our senses, including the sense of smell. Thank Him for taking pleasure today in our evangelism rather than in the aroma of the mixture of fragrant substances.**

ASK

Do you know any characteristics of God that start with the letter Q? Be sure everyone is speaking about God with reverence and respect. Here are some ideas for you.

QUICKENING
QUIET

Quiet

The quiet voice of God can be heard in silence.

Here is a story that has been told and retold many times. One day a farmer lost his watch in the hay barn. This watch had great value to the farmer because it had been a gift from his father. The farmer searched the barn inside and out, but to no avail. He searched for several hours before finally becoming exhausted. He noticed a few boys playing nearby, and he decided to ask them for help, promising a reward to the one who would find the watch lost in the hay.

When the boys heard about the reward, they rushed to the barn, shouting and each excited to be the one to claim the reward. They looked throughout the whole barn, but did not find anything either. The farmer was ready to give up hope and sent the crowd of boys away. But one small boy came to him and asked for another chance. The farmer agreed and sent the boy to the barn. To his utter surprise, after a short time, the boy brought him his lost watch! With great interest, the farmer asked the boy how he managed to find it.

ASK

How do you think the boy found the lost watch so quickly?

The boy told the farmer, "I didn't do anything special. I just sat on the floor and listened. In the silence, I heard the watch ticking, and I went where the sound was coming from. That's where I found the watch."

Our modern life is saturated with noise, and in order to hear God's voice, we need silence. Just like the boy found that valuable watch in silence, we can find precious fellowship with God in silence.

In 1 Kings 18, we read the exciting story of Elijah and the prophets of the false god Baal. (Note: if you have time, you might want to read through 1 Kings 18, especially verses 20–40.) After this exhilarating and exhausting day, Elijah fled from the wicked monarchs Ahab and Jezebel and finally ducked into a cave. The Lord said, "What are you doing here, Elijah?" (1 Kings 19:9). Elijah said he felt like he was the only faithful person left to speak for God.

ASK

Have you ever felt like you were the only person among your friends or in your class to be faithful to God?

God told Elijah to stand up on the mountain.

> The LORD passed by, and a mighty windstorm hit the moun-
> tain. It was such a terrible blast that the rocks were torn loose,
> but the LORD was not in the wind. After the wind there was an
> earthquake, but the LORD was not in the earthquake. And after
> the earthquake there was a fire, but the LORD was not in the
> fire. And after the fire there was the sound of a gentle whisper.
> —1 KINGS 19:11–12 NLT

The Lord was in the gentle whisper!

The Bible tells us that often Jesus went off alone to be quiet and pray (e.g., Matt. 14:23; Mark 1:35; Luke 6:12). This is a good example for us to follow, and perhaps where the term Quiet Time comes from. Sometimes we want the big moments, the loud, splashy, exciting encounters with God such as Elijah's miraculous time with the prophets of Baal. But often it's in the quiet that God speaks most "loudly" to us.

It is in the silence that we can hear the quiet voice of God today.

PRAYER | **Worship God, who values silence. Thank Him for His desire to reveal Himself to us and to direct us in our lives.**

ASK

Do you know any characteristics of God that start with the letter R?
Be sure everyone is speaking about God with reverence and respect. Here are some ideas for you.

RABBI (JESUS)
RADIANT
READER OF HEARTS
REAL
RECOGNIZABLE
RECORD HOLDER
REDEEMER
RELEVANT

RELIABLE
RESPECTED
RESPONSIVE
REVEALED
RICH
RIGHT
RIGHTEOUS
ROCK

Redeemer

God created you. He also redeemed you.

This story happened to a little boy who lived in a village on the shore of a big lake. One day he made a toy boat, and with great excitement went down to the lake to launch it. The boy lowered the ship into the water and began to observe. While his boat glided over the waves, a gust of wind pushed it to the middle of the lake, and it went out of sight. The boy was very upset. A few days later, he went through the village and saw his boat in the window of a local store.

ASK

What do you think happened after that?

Excited, the boy ran into the store and said to the owner, "Sir, that's my boat in your store window! It's mine! I made it myself!"

The owner replied, "I'm sorry, but I bought it from another boy who brought it here, so now it's mine. If you want it, you'll have to pay me."

The boy ran home and broke open his piggy bank. He went back to the store with all his money in his hand, and placed the required amount on the counter.

The storeowner went to the window, got the boat, and gave it to the boy. The boy lovingly embraced the boat, and as he left, he said, "Now you're mine twice. I made you *and* I bought you."[21]

This story is a great illustration of what Jesus did for us: He created us, *and* He bought us. That's what a redeemer does: buys back or pays a price. You might even think of someone held captive and being rescued when someone pays a ransom. And Jesus not only bought us back from being held captive to sin—Jesus *is* the ransom (Mark 10:45). He not only redeemed us, He is the redeemer.

The Bible says that God bought each of us for a price:

> You are not your own, for you were bought with a price.
> —1 CORINTHIANS 6:19–20

The price paid by God for us was the life of Jesus Christ. It is a very high price! This is why our hearts must always be filled with gratitude to God for His redemption.

PRAYER | **Worship God while meditating on His being our Redeemer and what that means. Thank Him for the fact that Jesus was willing to give His life for you. Thank God for the people who will learn about God's plan of salvation from you.**

SACRIFICIAL
SALVATION
SAVING
SEARCHER
   OF HEARTS
SEEKING
SHADDAI
SHIELD
SIGNIFICANT
SINLESS

SLOW
   (TO GET ANGRY)
SMART
SOVEREIGN
SPEAKING
SPIRIT
STRONG
SUN
SUPPORT

Sacrificial

Christ took the judgment so that you could live in freedom.

In the village of Marshaly in Sumy Region of Ukraine, a sixty-eight-year-old grandfather died from a lightning strike. The man was found covering his young grandson with his own body.

Andrei was twelve, and had always helped his grandfather herd cows. On that terrible day, they were caught in a thunder and lightning storm complete with hail. This is how Andrei recalls it.

"We were herding the cows. Then the rain started. We sat down, got to talking, then we walked, and then . . . I can't remember anything. I must have been knocked down. When I got up I saw my grandfather and I cried out, 'Grandpa! Grandpa!' But he just lay there, silent. He was lying face down. I turned him over on his back, and his eyes were open. He was completely black. I turned him back over because I was afraid."

Andrei said that he had turned his cellphone off before the storm began, but when he woke up, the phone was on. He immediately phoned his mother. Later, authorities discovered that the lightning had bizarrely struck the grandpa in his heart. The current passed though the kidney, hit Andrei's cellphone, and then passed through his grandfather's knee.

ASK

How did Andrei stay alive?

Perhaps you have guessed that his grandfather absorbed almost the entire electrical charge. He fell down and covered his beloved boy with his own body.[22]

This story reminds us of the work of Jesus Christ. He "covered" us with His own body from the just wrath of God:

> God showed his great love for us by sending Christ to die for us
> while we were still sinners. And since we have been made right
> in God's sight by the blood of Christ, he will certainly save us
> from God's condemnation.
> —ROMANS 5:8–9 NLT

The just and righteous wrath of God is like lightning. No man can measure up to God's requirements. What Jesus did on the cross was indeed a heroic deed. Because of His love for us, He sacrificially died for our sins, and then He rose again. Jesus "covered" us with Himself, and because of this, like Andrei, Christians are now alive in God's presence. On Judgment Day they will be covered by the sacrifice of Jesus too, because He took all the "charge" of God's righteous wrath.

PRAYER | **Worship the sacrificial Jesus Christ who gave His life for us. Thank the heavenly Father for His redemptive plan and for the high price paid by Jesus Christ.**

Do you know any characteristics of God that start with the letter T? Be sure everyone is speaking about God with reverence and respect. Here are some ideas for you.

TEACHER
TENDERHEARTED
THINKER
TIMELESS
TRANSFORMER
TREASURE
TRIUNE
TRUE

Triune

The Trinity gives us an example of perfect unity.

There was a famous theologian and philosopher named Aurelius Augustine who lived in the fourth century AD. He loved to meditate about God. He tried to comprehend God's triunity. "How can God be one, and still be three persons: Father, Son, and Holy Spirit?" Augustine could not find peace of mind because of all his reflections on the Trinity. According to tradition, one day he was walking along the seashore and saw a boy. Augustine watched the boy scoop water from the sea with a shell and pour it into a hole he dug in the sand. Augustine asked what the boy was doing. The boy answered,

"I want to scoop the whole sea into this hole!"

ASK

What do you think Augustine said?

Augustine smiled and said that it was not possible. Right then he realized that he himself had been acting exactly like this boy in trying to comprehend the Trinity, the inexhaustible mystery of God.[23]

Even though the word "Trinity" is never used in the Bible, we clearly see the triunity of God in this passage of the Old Testament. The speaker is the Servant-Messiah, Jesus:[24]

> "Draw near to me, hear this: from the beginning I have not
> spoken in secret, from the time it came to be I have been there."
> And now the Lord GOD has sent me, and his Spirit.
> —ISAIAH 48:16

Notice how the Messiah (Jesus Christ) says here that He had been sent by the Lord God (the Father) and His Spirit (the Holy Spirit). The Father, the Son, and the Holy Spirit do everything together in complete harmony with one another.

We will never be able to comprehend the Trinity, but everything that we do understand about the Trinity is an example of unity. God himself is triune, and He desires the same unity in our families and our churches. Quarrels and conflicts destroy unity, which is why we should avoid them and keep peace among ourselves.

Think about harmony in the function of our eyes. Both of our eyes move simultaneously in complete harmony.

ASK

Try looking up with one eye and down with the other. *Can you do it?*

No, it doesn't work! Our eyes are connected in a strong unity. Because of this unity, we can see with visual depth. In the same way, our triune Lord wants us to take care of each other and to guard our unity against conflicts and quarrels.

People from the very beginning of the Christian church tried to describe the Trinity. Some of the church fathers (early church leaders) found a way to describe the relationship of the Father, the Son, and the Holy Spirit using the sun. Think of God the Father as the sun. The sun's job is to give light to the earth (Gen. 1:14–19). The radiance that flows from the sun, Jesus—think of it as God the Son—is the light of the world (Heb. 1:3; John 1:9–10; 8:12). And we can think of the heat that comes from the sun as the Holy Spirit. [25]

Light, radiance, heat—a good picture of God the Father, God the Son, God the Holy Spirit. Nothing we can think of can perfectly describe the triune God, but maybe we can understand it a little better now.

PRAYER | **Worship the triune God, who cannot be comprehended by our human minds. Thank God for His unity and for helping us live in unity with each other.**

Do you know any characteristics of God that start with the letter U? Be sure everyone is speaking about God with reverence and respect. Here are some ideas for you.

UNCHANGEABLE
UNIQUE
UNSTOPPABLE

Unchangeable

God's love is even stronger than the love of a mother.

There is a parable told by a Mr. Lopatin. He calls it "The Most Constant Love." It goes like this: Once upon a time there was a famous philosopher. You probably know that a philosopher is someone who likes to think and discuss and debate.

This philosopher invited some friends to his house. They started talking about whether things are always changing or if some things just stay the same. Pretty soon the discussion grew rather heated. Half the people said that everything in this world is always changing. One person explained. She said, "Look, think of a rich person. One day he has everything he could want—including lots of friends or so-called friends—but the next day he might lose all his possessions and money and no one wants to be his friend anymore."

"I agree," another said. "Think of a beautiful estate with many rooms, which took decades to build. It's filled with ornate furniture, and surrounded by acres of trees. Then a terrible fire comes and destroys it. In an instant, the whole place goes up in a blaze and it's gone."

"You're absolutely right," someone else said. "Even the strong rocks of the mountains can be eroded. So even they are changing."

But some of the philosopher's friends did not agree. One man said, "What about things you can't see? Feelings such as kindness and love do not have to change. What about memories of pleasant times? These are permanent." But still, those who believed everything is always changing stuck to their belief. One said, "Even feelings and emotions and memories do not last. They too can change and be forgotten."

ASK

What do you believe to be constant and unchangeable in our world? Let's think of some examples.

The lively discussion in the philosopher's house went on until his mother came into the room with some fruit and iced tea. After she served refreshments, she affectionately placed her hand on her son's shoulder. And the philosopher suddenly exclaimed, "I know something that *never* changes: a mother's love!"

And all his guests agreed.

This is how Mr. Lopatin's parable ends, but we as Christians should add something to these words. The parable's author didn't mention any cases where mothers abandon their children. So sadly, yes, in some cases, even a mother's love can falter or fail, but these situations are rare. God knows all about how powerful maternal love is, but He also knows about abandoned children. He says even if a mother could forget her children, God will never, never forget His. His Word tells us,

> Can a mother forget her nursing child? Can she feel no love for the child she has borne? But even if that were possible, I would not forget you!
> —ISAIAH 49:15 NLT

God's love to us is 100 percent unchangeable and constant! "Jesus Christ is the same yesterday and today and forever" (Heb. 13:8). Glory be to Him!

PRAYER | Worship God while meditating on how He is unchangeable and constant in His love for each of us. Thank Him for taking care of you daily.

VALIANT
VIGILANT
VIVACIOUS
VOCIFEROUS
VOCATIONAL
  (HE'S ALWAYS
  WORKING; HE'S
  THE CREATOR OF
  WORK)

Vociferous

The voice of the Lord is powerful and full of majesty.

Let's say this word: vociferous. It's a lot to roll off the tongue, isn't it?

What does it mean? Well, to get us started, the word vociferous comes from the Latin word *vox*, which means voice. So vociferous has something to do with a voice.

What kind of voice? Vociferous can mean strident, boisterous, and other similar impressions. And it also has positive meanings such as expressive, plain-spoken, blunt, expressive, forceful, zealous, emphatic.

Let's think of different voices: the voice of a mother, the voice of a loved one, the voice of a boss, the voice of a teacher, the voice of a friend. Each of these voices call up certain associations in us. By their voices we recognize the ones we care about. Sometimes a person's voice or tone tells us something about their character: a rough voice, a gentle voice, and so on.

ASK

What kind of voice do you think God has?

There is a song in the Bible, Psalm 29, and the main theme of that song is the voice of God. Here's what we learn from this poetic passage:

> The voice of the LORD is over the waters;
>> the God of glory thunders,
>> the LORD, over many waters.
> The voice of the LORD is powerful;
>> the voice of the LORD is full of majesty.
>
> The voice of the LORD breaks the cedars;
>> the LORD breaks the cedars of Lebanon.
> —PSALM 29:3–5

To have a better understanding of the power of God's voice, think about this: a cedar of Lebanon is a mighty tree reaching 140–160 feet high, about as tall as a fifteen-story building. Its trunk is about eight feet around, so it would take three adults to clasp their hands around it. And the psalmist says that with his voice, the Lord splinters these cedars like shingles!

> He makes Lebanon to skip like a calf,
>> and Sirion like a young wild ox.
> The voice of the LORD flashes forth flames of fire.
> The voice of the LORD shakes the wilderness;
>> the LORD shakes the wilderness of Kadesh.
> —PSALM 29:6–8

The words "The voice of the LORD flashes forth flames of fire" create an imagery of a severe thunderstorm with lightning. Then it says that "the voice of the LORD . . . shakes the wilderness of Kadesh." Perhaps this verse describes a gale-force wind blowing from the mountains in the North to the area of Kadesh (in the South), where it lifts the sand particles and propels sand dunes, creating the impression of a shaking desert.

The voice of the LORD . . . strips the forests bare, and in his
temple all cry, "Glory!"
—PSALM 29:9

Oak wood is characterized by high durability, and it cannot be bent in the
same way as, for example, birch or pine. In these words, we see the image of a
strong hurricane that strips trees of their leaves and bends oaks. Such a phenomenon occurs only during very powerful gusts of wind! According to the psalmist,
the voice of God is so vociferous (think of loud, intense, forceful) that it produces
powerful hurricanes!

ASK

How is vociferous a good word to describe God?

Noël Piper, author and wife of Bible teacher John Piper, wrote this poem
about a devastating hurricane:

> God strode the beach
>> Our legs and faces could not bear the piercing, blasting sand
> God stepped ashore
>> Palms, waves, scattering branches in his path
> God strode inland
>> Magnolias, pines and oaks who had stretched a hundred
>>> years toward God fell to the ground before him
> God stood and breathed, while we in the dark, closed closet
>> feared to face his glory[26]

ASK

We see that God speaks through nature. *How else does God speak
to us?*

PRAYER | Worship the Great and Vociferous God while meditating on His voice. Thank Him for preferring to speak to us today through the Bible in the quietness of our hearts.

Do you know any characteristics of God that start with the letter W? Be sure everyone is speaking about God with reverence and respect. Here are some ideas for you.

WAY
WEIGHING
WHOLE
WISDOM-GIVER
WISE
WONDERFUL
WORD

Way

Every one of us needs the way to God. Jesus is this Way.

In the year of 1934, in a small Indian village, a boy named Dashrath Manjhi was born; he later became famous all over the country. He lived all of his life in the village of Gehlaur among ordinary people. Their village was so poor that they didn't even have a hospital there. If they had a sickness or an injury, the people had to travel a long and difficult road to the nearest town where they could receive medical services. A huge stony hill separated the small village from the larger town. To get to the larger town, people had to travel for more than 45 miles all the way around the mountain over a sandy road.

On one fateful day, Dashrath's beloved wife deeply wounded her foot. Because of the long distance to the hospital, she wasn't able to receive immediate help, and sadly, she died. Grieved by his loss, Dashrath decided that no one else in his village should experience such a tragedy.

ASK

What do you think Dashrath did?

He decided to get rid of the stone barrier that divided the village and the neighboring town. He made an appeal to the local government, but was refused any assistance in that endeavor.

In 1960, Dashrath collected all the tools he needed and went to the hill to carve a shortcut through it. Every day he went there as if it was his day job, and he dug, shoveled, and removed the stones. People called him crazy because the task before him simply seemed impossible. Dashrath worked daily for twenty-two years, one day at a time. His hard work came to completion in 1982: he carved a passageway through the hill, and it was 360 feet long, 30 feet wide, and almost 26 feet deep.

Thanks to this new passageway, the overall distance between the small village and the larger town decreased to just a few miles, which brought incredible relief to the local community. When people travel over this new pass, they remember Dashrath Manjhi's diligence and perseverance. Today all of India knows about that persistent farmer who was nicknamed "Mountain Man" by the people. His story was covered in several movies, which made him known around the world.

This story about the hill in India reminds us about another mountain: the mountain that is not between towns but is the barrier between God and human beings—the insurmountable mountain of human sin. It separates sinful people from the Holy God. It cannot be carved through by means of good works, nor even by following God's commandments.

God commanded the Jews to make a veil in the temple to serve as a visual reminder of the barrier of sin for His people. The people of the Bible knew that there is no direct way to the Holy God—there's simply none! The wide massive veil was woven from dense thread, and was like a wall that separated the place of God's presence from anyone who attended the temple. It hung in the temple for hundreds of years, pointing to the separation between the Holy God and us sinners.

It would have been so even now, if it wasn't for Jesus' coming to this world. With His death on the cross, He carved for us the way to God. He could confidently say of Himself,

"I am the way, and the truth, and the life. No one comes to the Father except through me."
—JOHN 14:6

Just as Dashrath Manjhi carved the pass through the hill, Jesus Christ paved the direct way to God through our insurmountable mountain of sins. He died on the cross, and every human being who believes in the sacrifice of Jesus receives complete forgiveness of their sins. In God's forgiveness, the mountain that separates us from God melts down. Therefore, Jesus Himself is the Way to God for every believer.

In the moment of the crucifixion of Jesus, something strange happened to the veil in the temple—it was torn: "The curtain of the temple was torn in two, from top to bottom" (Mark 15:38).

God decided to show all people that there is now a new Way through that impenetrable mountain of sin. Through faith in Jesus Christ, every Christian has God's help and support available to them. Just like that Indian village now has medical care readily available, every believer in Jesus gets timely assistance from God.

The residents of that Indian village are still grateful to their fellow countryman for the way he made for them, and in the same way Christians praise God for Jesus Christ, their Way to God.

PRAYER | **Worship Jesus, who is your Way to God. Praise Him for becoming available to every human being.**

ASK

Do you know any characteristics of God that start with the letter X? Be sure everyone is speaking about God with reverence and respect. Here is one idea for you.

Xenial

Our God is kind, cordial, and inviting.

We don't have a lot of ordinary words in English that start with X, do we? There's X-ray . . . and maybe X-ray reminds us of how God can see right through us!

Sometimes we think of words that start with the sound of an X: excellent, expert, extraordinary. These also are good descriptions of God.

But let's learn a brand-new word that starts with X but actually has a Z sound: xenial (*zee* nee ul). This word means being hospitable, especially with foreigners or with people you don't know.

The Lord is xenial. And you and I are invited to fellowship with the Lord Himself!

Warren Buffett is a very rich American whose wealth has been estimated at over $67 billion. There have been auctions where people could bid to have lunch with him.

ASK

How much do you think people are willing to pay to have lunch with Warren Buffett?

One time the starting bid for a lunch with Mr. Buffet was set at $25,000. On another occasion, two businessmen paid $650,000 for such an opportunity. And yet another time, a Chinese businessman, Mr. Zhu Ye, paid $2.35 million at a charity auction to have lunch with Mr. Buffett. Sometime later, a woman who chose to remain anonymous paid almost $3.5 million to have lunch with Mr. Buffett! The people who were willing to spend such money for lunch were not paying merely for food, as grand and gourmet as these meals were, but rather for being in the presence of a great billionaire, and the opportunity to converse with him.

But in the Bible, we read of something even more amazing. The Almighty Himself invited seventy-four men, and they didn't have to pay Him anything! We read about this great cordiality of God in the book of Exodus:

> Then Moses, Aaron, Nadab, Abihu, and the seventy elders of
> Israel climbed up the mountain. There they saw the God of Is-
> rael. Under his feet there seemed to be a surface of brilliant blue
> lapis lazuli, as clear as the sky itself. And though these nobles of
> Israel gazed upon God, he did not destroy them. In fact, they
> ate a covenant meal, eating and drinking in his presence!
> —EXODUS 24:9–11 NLT

And today our heavenly Father remains just as xenial. Do you remember what xenial means? It means hospitable, friendly, and accommodating, especially to strangers and foreigners. The Lord Himself invites us to fellowship with His heavenly family and with His Son:

> God is faithful, by whom you were called into the fellowship of
> his Son, Jesus Christ our Lord.
> —1 CORINTHIANS 1:9

While inviting us, God also expects us to tell our friends about His kindness. Unfortunately, so many of them view God as boring and picky rather than cordial and xenial. Let us be good witnesses to the true and inviting character of God.

ASK

How can we imitate God and be xenial?

PRAYER | **Worship God for His openness and xenial cordiality. Thank Him for His wide embrace that is ready to encompass the whole world. Which of your friends do you need to tell about God's cordiality?**

Do you know any characteristics of God that start with the letter Y?
Be sure everyone is speaking about God with reverence and respect. Here are some ideas for you.

YESHUA
YHWH (YAHWEH)
YHWH-ELOHIM
YHWH-JIREH
YHWH-MEKADDISHKEM (MEKADDISH)
YHWH-NISSI

YHWH-ROREH (RAPHA)
YHWH-ROHI
YHWH-SABAOTH
YHWH-SHALOM
YHWH-SHAMMAH
YHWH-TSIDKENU

YHWH (Yahweh)

*God's name: we know how it is spelled,
but we don't know how it sounds.*

Let's each write down our names with no vowels.

ASK

How is the name of God spelled with no vowels?

In Hebrew the name of God was spelled without vowels, and it looked like this: יהוה (YHWH). It was the name that the Lord revealed Himself with to Moses:

> God said to Moses, "I AM WHO I AM." And he said, "Say this to the people of Israel: 'I AM has sent me to you.'"
> —EXODUS 3:14

In this particular translation, the word YHWH is rendered as "I AM." *What does this name mean?* "I AM" means "I am the One who exists." With His name, the Lord emphasizes that He is the only real living God.

How does this name sound? People know how the name of God is spelled, but its pronunciation is a mystery not revealed to anyone, because all we have are consonants. The word YHWH was never pronounced out loud, as it was prohibited due to the great reverence toward God. Only the high priest pronounced it once a year, and only in the holy of holies in the temple. So, for example, if a person who had never heard the name "Nicolas" saw the name spelled as "NCLS," they could add some arbitrary vowels and render the name as "Nucolis," or "Nacoles." That is the reason why nowadays the name of God is pronounced in various ways: Yahweh, Jehovah, Yehowah.

Who else has such a name? The name YHWH belongs only to God, and no creature has a right to liken itself to God! Despite the strict prohibition, Jesus Christ applied this name to Himself. On one occasion the religious leaders nearly killed Him because of it (see John 10:22–33). What gave Him the right to apply YHWH, the prohibited name of God, to Himself? There's only one answer: Jesus Christ is the "I AM," the living God.

A kaleidoscope is a bright and fascinating object. It looks like a telescope from the outside, but there are mirrors and pieces of colored glass inside that are used to create a variety of visual mosaics. As soon as you rotate the kaleidoscope, the mosaic pattern changes into a surprisingly new form.

In the Bible we are given a true kaleidoscope of God's attributes through the name of God, YHWH.

These can be called the facets of God's name. For example, "YHWH-Rapha" means "the LORD who heals." "I am the LORD, your healer" (Ex. 15:26).

And there are many other examples of God using various names to describe Himself. Why does God show us so many shades of His name? One of the reasons is to give us comfort. Each trait reflects God's character and is an answer to people's basic needs of protection, healing, and assistance. Here are meanings of some of God's names in Hebrew:

YHWH-Jireh means "the LORD will provide." (Gen. 22:14)

YHWH-Nissi means "the LORD Is My Banner."(Ex. 17:15)

YHWH-Mekaddishkem (Mekaddish) means "I am the LORD who sanctifies you." (Lev. 20:8)

YHWH-Shalom means "the LORD Is Peace." (Judg. 6:24)

YHWH-Elohim means "the LORD God made the earth and the heavens." (Gen. 2:4)

YHWH-Tsidkenu means "the LORD is our righteousness." (Jer. 23:6; 33:16)

YHWH-Rohi means "the LORD is my shepherd." (Ps. 23:1)

YHWH-Shammah means "the LORD Is There" (Ezek. 48:35)

YHWH-Sabaoth means "the LORD of hosts." (Isa. 1:24)

PRAYER | **Worship God while meditating on His multifaceted character. Thank Him for the "kaleidoscope" of His attributes and traits, and that by knowing them we can find comfort and support in Him. And thank Him for revealing Himself to us in Jesus Christ in a way we can understand.**

ASK

Do you know any characteristics of God that start with the letter Z? Be sure everyone is speaking about God with reverence and respect. Here is an idea for you.

Zealous

God is passionate about your salvation.

Who would have thought that the cliff called the Gap on Australia's Pacific coast would become famous not because of its beauty, but because of the constant tragedies that happen there? Since the nineteenth century, people who have decided to commit suicide come to this sad place. According to statistics, no fewer than fifty people a year end their lives here by leaping off the cliff. It was so until a former Navy seaman named Don Ritchie, nicknamed the Angel of the Gap by the locals, settled on the cliff.

The windows in Mr. Ritchie's house in Sydney faced the Pacific coast. Every day Don stood and intently watched through his window, but not for the love of the beautiful view. He was saving the ones who decided to commit suicide. For fifty years, he watched people on the cliff, and every time he noticed something wrong, he would rush to the rescue. Before leaping off, people would timidly walk along the cliff coming closer and closer to the edge. And in that moment, Don would approach the stranger and start a conversation.

ASK

What do you think would happen after that?

This is how Don described his method of rescue. "I would just slowly walk up and smile. I would ask, 'Is there something I can do to help you?'" By that time the person was usually sitting on the very edge, and their bag, and their note, and anything else they had with them was placed behind—they were ready to jump at any moment. Don would calmly invite them to his house for a cup of tea—and many would agree. And that was Don's very goal, to give the person a bit of time, to give them an opportunity to understand, and then the next morning things might not seem as gloomy.

That was his purpose—saving people. In 2010 Don was awarded the Medal of the Order of Australia for his service to the community by preventing suicide, and was named Citizen of the Year for 2010. In 2011 he was named the Australian Local Hero of the Year. People saved by Don often sent him letters of gratitude even ten or twenty years after their encounter on the cliff. Don Ritchie lived to be 86 years old and died in May 2012. Over the years of his life, he officially saved 164 people from suicide, but his family says that in reality the number of the rescued was much higher—more than 400 people![27] The life of this man and his passion for saving people is truly inspiring.

But God is even more passionate than Don about the salvation of human souls. He so loved the world that He gave His Son Jesus Christ, so that every human being who believes in Him could have eternal life. Don offered people a cup of tea—but God offers salvation in Jesus Christ, who gives Living Water. Jesus has a great multitude of saved souls among all tribes and peoples. Please take note of God's passionate desire to save every human on the earth:

> God our Savior, who desires all people to be saved and to come
> to the knowledge of the truth.
> —1 TIMOTHY 2:3–4

The words "all people" mean every human being on this earth. Every human being in your city. God wants to save every one of your relatives, every neighbor in your town, and every student in your class. God is passionate about it!

> The Lord is not slow to fulfill his promise as some count slowness, but is patient toward you, not wishing that any should perish, but that all should reach repentance.
> —2 PETER 3:9

One episode from the life of Christ gives us a vivid description of His passion for saving people. The Jerusalem temple was a place where all people could worship God. A part of the temple courtyard was called the Court of the Gentiles. This court was the only place in the whole temple where anyone who wasn't a Jew could enter. And it was provided not only for them to behold the beauty of the temple, but to give people an opportunity to pray and honor God. God appointed this court for His "date" with representatives of other nations. If we lived back then, the Court of the Gentiles would be designated for us.

But what did Jews do? They kept their own court sacred with all reverence, but in the Court of the Gentiles, they installed trade booths. Currency exchange, animal trade, market bustle, greed, and deceit filled that place. Praying in such a noisy place became impossible. Rather than a place of prayer, it had become a place where money-changers were—not to provide people with the animal sacrifices they needed, but to make a profit. People who looked for God's presence could not find it there any longer. It angered Jesus! He made a whip out of ropes and started to zealously turn over the tables:

> And Jesus entered the temple and drove out all who sold and bought in the temple, and he overturned the tables of the money-changers and the seats of those who sold pigeons.
> —MATTHEW 21:12

Just as Don couldn't indifferently watch people give in to suicide, Jesus could not indifferently observe the trade that prevented people from seeking God and praying. The holy zeal of Christ was manifested in His anger against the merchants who were a barrier for the Gentiles. Even today, this zealous God wants to save all people in every nation so He can share eternity with us in intimate fellowship.

PRAYER | **Worship God, who is very passionate about the salvation of your relatives and friends. Thank Jesus Christ that His passion and zeal (intense enthusiasm) are not growing any weaker, and thank Him for His desire, that is as passionate as it was at the temple, to have close fellowship with all people.**

PART THREE

LASTING
TREASURES

CHAPTER 5

Time to Cut the Umbilical Cord

THE TIME OF FAMILY WORSHIP is very important, but it is also important to remember what we discussed in chapter 2, "God and Worshiping Him." Let us refresh those words in our minds:

> The best thing you as parents can do for the spiritual life of your children is provide them with opportunities to go on a "date with God in the Bible's pages," and then encourage them to follow God's revelation.

Providing our children with opportunities for a date with God is a necessary task that we are capable of as parents. On our shoulders, we parents carry the responsibility of not only family evenings, but of helping our children arrange their personal time with God.

One day, our family was sitting at the table having breakfast. A family with two young girls was staying over at our house. Bit by bit our conversation shifted to the subject of quiet time with God and with our children. From the conversation, they learned that I have my quiet time daily at 6:30 in the morning. This has been my habit for many years. Morning quiet time with Jesus is the basis of my spiritual life. My daughter gets up a bit later and spends time with God on her own, I explained.

"Great, and how old is she?" they asked me.

"Eleven."

It was obvious that my answer surprised them slightly. Having time with God at such an early age has history in our family. On one occasion I visited a church minister who shared with me that he reads the Bible with his daughter before she goes to school. Such an approach seemed new to me. My family took that idea and decided to try it out for ourselves. At that time Anna was nine, and we started to spend quiet time together in the morning. Ten to fifteen minutes was enough time to read a small passage from the New Testament out loud and to pray. I chose a translation of the New Testament that was understandable for my daughter (praise God, we now have plenty of translations to choose from); each chapter was split into smaller portions. We continued that way for over a year. In the summer it was more sporadic, but in the fall, when school started again, we resumed the habit, making it a daily part of our lives.

Some people hold the opinion that parents should read the Bible together with their children on a daily basis, but it is quite appropriate to ask ourselves, "Until what age should we do it?" At some point I felt that my daughter was too dependent on me for this quiet time. She would even skip it if I happened to oversleep or be away at a morning meeting with someone. It wasn't an easy decision, but I suggested that she keep on spending time with God, but now on her own.

"Sweetheart, I want you to spend your own quiet time with Jesus, starting this morning. We have been doing it together for quite a while, and now you are capable of hearing His voice and praying in the morning by yourself."

"Dad, I want to spend this time with you, just as we did before."

I realized how difficult that transition would be for her, but understanding its importance made me steadfast in the decision I made. I tried to comfort her.

"Honey, the moment has come when this time needs to become personal for you and for me. Why don't we share our thoughts and reflections from this time while I take you to school?"

She agreed. That was a moment when I as a father cut her "umbilical cord" of dependence on me in her quiet time with God. Every obstetrician knows how important it is to cut the umbilical cord of a newborn child at just the right time so that the child can eat and breathe on its own. Of course, it cannot be done while the child is still in the mother's womb, but it is crucial to know the right moment to do it. Jesus left His disciples at just the right time, even though they were upset (see John 14:1–4). The apostle Paul, having served in Ephesus for three years, left new elders (see Acts 20:31–32). Genuine biblical discipleship is impossible without the timely release of disciples from one's caring hands. This is what I mean: parents have the responsibility in their families to lead each of their children in their own personal relationship with Christ.

A few days after the breakfast conversation, I was visiting a missionary family from Papua New Guinea. Eugene told me that his son had been spending personal private time with Jesus since he was eight. When he said that, he showed me his son's Bible, which had verses highlighted and underlined in different colors. It was my turn to be surprised! If your children take their first independent steps in their lives, it is high time to teach them about personal fellowship with God.

CHAPTER 6

Why I Don't Pray "Lord, Bless This Food" Anymore

MOST OF THE CHRISTIANS I know have usually started the grace before a meal with something like, "Lord, bless this food . . ." I also prayed using these words until I met someone who convinced me to reconsider this practice. If you are one of those who "bless the food" in your prayers, this chapter is for you!

This is not about people's habits of praying; after all, some people are accustomed to praying in one way, and others are accustomed to praying in a different way. But the issue of what kind of prayer should be said before meals is much more important and deeper than it may seem on the surface. This is because it concerns not only food, but also the upbringing of the next generation. Let's take a look at this subject together.

In the Old Testament God gave Israel the following commandment:

> When you have eaten your fill, be sure to praise the LORD your
> God for the good land he has given you.
> **—DEUTERONOMY 8:10** NLT

Here it says: "When you have eaten . . . praise the LORD for the good land He has given you." The Scripture called on the Jews to give thanks to the Lord for the blessings they have received, including their food and the good land from which it came. Since those times and even now, devout Jewish people say a prayer called the *hamotzi*, "the blessing of the bread,"[28] but what is even more important, it's not the bread that is blessed, but as stated in the verse we just read, it is God Himself who is blessed. This is obvious for every Jew: to thank the Lord, the Giver of the food, before the meal. That is why the Jews have different blessings for food, each beginning with the words "Blessed are You, O Lord our God, King of the universe, who brings forth bread from the earth!" Said in Hebrew, it is: *Baruch Atah Adonai Eloheinu Melech ha'olam ha'motzi lechem min ha'aretz* (you can find the pronunciation of this prayer online—you might even want to memorize it!).

There are blessings for the bread, for grains, for wine and grape juice, and for fruits, vegetables, and all other foods.[29] Every meal eaten in a Jewish family is accompanied by the glorification of God and thanksgiving to Him. In the New Testament, on several occasions, Jesus Christ prayed before the meal:

> Then he ordered the crowds to sit down on the grass, and taking the five loaves and the two fish, he looked up to heaven and said a blessing. Then he broke the loaves and gave them to the disciples, and the disciples gave them to the crowds.
> —MATTHEW 14:19; SEE ALSO MARK 6:41

Some people are mistaken and think that the word "blessing" in these texts refers to the bread, but in fact, the Jews did not bless the bread itself, but blessed God, the Giver, and offered Him their thanks.[30]

> As they were eating, he took bread, and after blessing it broke it and gave it to them, and said, "Take; this is my body."
> —MARK 14:22

Though we read that Jesus blessed the bread, we must remember that the bread symbolized Christ's body, which was soon to be sacrificed for our sins. Jesus was not adding in a request, such as "bless the bread," as we might when we say grace before a meal, but reminding His apostles—and us—to observe this sacrament to remember Him. We can say that Jesus was, in effect, blessing Himself in this blessing of the bread. Paul recalls Christ's prayer at the Last Supper:

> For I received from the Lord what I also delivered to you, that
> the Lord Jesus on the night when he was betrayed took bread,
> and when he had given thanks, he broke it, and said, "This is my
> body, which is for you. Do this in remembrance of me."
> —1 CORINTHIANS 11:23–24

To the apostle Paul, who was a Jew, it was evident that Jesus gave thanks to God for that bread. That is why Paul wrote "took bread, and when he had given thanks . . ." Obviously, He had given thanks to God, not to the bread. In the same way, the word "blessed" in terms of the prayer before a meal must always refer to God.

In the New Testament, the prayer before a meal is always a prayer of thanksgiving and praise to God:

> If I partake with thankfulness, why am I denounced because of
> that for which I give thanks?
> —1 CORINTHIANS 10:30

God gives us good and perfect gifts (James 1:17), including food to nourish our bodies. Some people twist Scripture to try to make it mean something other than it does—for example, that some people should not get married, or that certain foods should be avoided on a certain day of the week. But these are man-made rules. God's Word is clear that everything He made is good and that we should be thankful to Him for His provision:

> [Some] forbid marriage and require abstinence from foods that
> God created to be received with thanksgiving by those who be-
> lieve and know the truth. For everything created by God is good,
> and nothing is to be rejected if it is received with thanksgiving,
> for it is made holy by the word of God and prayer.
> —1 TIMOTHY 4:3–5

Here we read that a prayer before meals is a prayer of thanksgiving. And food "is made holy by the word of God and prayer." That is right, but by what prayer? By a prayer of thanksgiving, my friends. This is not the time for a prayer of request. This text does not give us any grounds for asking God, who gave us food, to bless and sanctify this food as well, but it encourages us to thank the Creator for the food. It is also said here that food "is made holy by the word of God and prayer" as a result of our thanksgiving prayer.

Let's look at what Jesus said when He fed the multitude.

> And taking the five loaves and the two fish, he looked up to heaven and said a blessing over them. Then he broke the loaves and gave them to the disciples to set before the crowd.
> —LUKE 9:16

That's right, Jesus "said a blessing over" the bread, but now we have a better understanding of what that means. He gave thanks to God for the loaves, and in this way He "blessed" them.

Sometimes we pray over our meals with a rote prayer, repeating the same words without giving much thought to what they mean. I am not saying that it's wrong to recite a prayer—there are many worthy prayers in the Bible we can use word-for-word or as a model for prayer. And Christians throughout the ages have recorded prayers that we may certainly feel free to read and to pray as our own.[31] What I am emphasizing is that saying grace over a meal should be a time to be thankful for what God has given us, rather than to turn it into a request, even one that sounds as simple as "please bless this food."

THE ISSUE IS MORE SERIOUS THAN IT SEEMS

Is the difference that important? For some, it's just a matter of semantics. But for me and my family, there is a deeper reason why this subject is so important and why I raised this topic. "Bless this food" is a human-centered prayer. In its nature, such a prayer is about ourselves, in my opinion, and the main focus is on our own well-being and safety. You may not agree, and perhaps this seems too strong of a statement, but it sounds to me like a prayer of a heathen. I'm not saying that asking God for His blessings is wrong (for God allows us to ask for His blessings; see, for example, Numbers 6:22–27), and of course it's right to thank God for the blessings He gives us, but the key point is this: *who* is in the center of our request to sanctify the food, and what are the motives for this request? It is obvious that the daily practice of such a prayer only encourages the consumer attitude toward God.

As opposed to our tendency to be self-centered, the Creator is in the center of the "blessed is the Lord" prayer. Such prayers exalt and glorify the Giver and serve as a good exercise for our hearts to give thanks to the Creator and worship Him.

The main point is this: what environments are our kids brought up in? After all, eating takes place several times a day, and what they hear at the table, more than anything else, shapes their understanding of God! Think about this: we pray before meals twenty times more often than we listen to Sunday sermons. This may be the reason why, in churches, we mostly hear the prayers of requests. Consumerism in our culture is formed by several factors, and praying with re-quests—drop by drop, day in and day out—is one key way self-centeredness has infected our faith. It often seems that it takes a special day like Thanksgiving to remind ourselves of the importance of gratitude to God. It is difficult to argue against this point and say that these things are not relevant.

As a result of a thorough study on this subject, I questioned my previous practice of praying at the table and began to pray in a new way: "We thank you, Lord, for the food You have given us. We praise You for Your kindness and gen-erosity. Amen." Now every prayer before breakfast, lunch, and supper has trans-formed from a regular request into our family worship to God. The question is not about the way you are used to praying, the question is—who is in the center of your prayer? And how do your words affect the people around you?

CHAPTER 7

A Prized Collection

I CAN'T BE the same anymore. In my life, I have developed an unusual habit of collecting truths about God. Whenever I come across a thought about God during my Bible reading, I title it and write it down in my notebook. It might look something like this:

Progressive

God reveals Himself to an individual gradually, more and more each time (see Ex. 6:3).

Contrastive

The hand of our God is for good on all who seek him, and the power of his wrath is against all who forsake him.
—EZRA 8:22

The same happens when I read Christian books. There was a time when I could read books without taking notes, but not anymore. A passion for knowing God leaves me restless. As I read books, I find more and more thoughts about God:

Uncreated

The human mind, being created, has an understandable un-easiness about the Uncreated. We do not find it comfortable to allow for the presence of One who is wholly outside of the circle of our familiar knowledge.[32]

—A. W. Tozer, *The Knowledge of the Holy*

Sociable

He actually enjoys having us speak to him. Developing a relationship with us is God's goal, and answers to prayer are a means he uses to foster self-disclosure, growth and understanding of both him and ourselves.[33]

—W. Bingham Hunter, *The God Who Hears*

Unwittingly I became a collector of God's attributes and qualities. Adam and Eve had a holistic view of God. They were given the treasure of knowing God as He is. After the fall, the world collapsed and crumbled, along with our view of God. While reading the Word of God, each one of us is to collect our own treasures of the knowledge of God. This is a task for us and for our children.

If you have worked through *Kitchen Table Devotions* (daily or weekly), you, too, will never be the same! A prized collection is now in your hands, and you'll want to add to it your thoughts of God. Or, in other words, acknowledging God will have become a daily part of your life. This is what the Word of God calls us to:

In all your ways acknowledge him, and he will make straight your paths.

—PROVERBS 3:6

There are multiple ways to fulfill this call of God in practice, and I hope that *Kitchen Table Devotions* has become a good tool for it. How many treasures have you found today? The key to keep finding more is already in your hands.

Notes

1. A. W. Tozer, *The Knowledge of the Holy* (© 1961), in *Three Spiritual Classics in One Volume* (Chicago: Moody, 2006), 198.

2. Bob Sjogren and Gerald Robison, *Cat & Dog Theology: Rethinking Our Relationship with Our Master* (Downers Grove, IL: InterVarsity Press, 2003), 37.

3. Ron Man, "Worship and the Glory of God," *Reformation and Revival* 9, no. 2 (Spring 2000): 84. Retrieved from https://biblicalstudies.org.uk/pdf/ref-rev/09-2/9-2_man1.pdf.

4. Exactly so: worship is possible in the midst of both work and school. Philip Yancey shares a testimony of Sara, a university student: "While studying for a graduate degree, I often wondered how to integrate the academic work with God. I found a quote from Abraham Joshua Heschel which I propped up on my desk: 'The school is a sanctuary . . . learning is a form of worship.'" *Prayer: Does It Make Any Difference?* (Grand Rapids: Zondervan, 2006), 61.

5. A. W. Tozer, *The Best of A. W. Tozer: Book Two,* compiled by Warren Wiersbe (Camp Hill, PA: WingSpread Publishers, 2007), 284.

6. Ibid.

7. Donald S. Whitney, *Spiritual Disciplines for the Christian Life*, revised and updated edition (Colorado Springs: NavPress, 2014), 107.

8. Ibid.

9. "About Papau New Guinea," Laszlo Mission League, https://laszlomission league.com/about-hauna-papau-new-guinea/.

10. Wycliffe Canada, "Papa's God Talk," September 5, 2019, https://www.wycliffe.ca/2019/09/05/papa-gods-talk/.

11. Don Richardson, "How Missionaries Enrich Cultures," *Evangelical Friend* 25, no. 6 (July/August 1992). Don Richardson told of the Yali and other Indonesian people in his book *Lords of the Earth* (Ventura, CA: Regal Books, 1977). He also authored the missions classics *Peace Child* and *Eternity in Their Hearts.*

12. Based on a story taken from H. Pryhodko, *Life Lessons* (Lutsk, Ukraine: Khrysty-ianske Zhyttia, 2009), 14.

13. Mary Whelchel, *Soaring on High: Spiritual Insights from the Life of an Eagle* (Chicago: Moody, 2001), 15.

14. Ibid., 11.

15. Ibid., 14.

16. James Romm, ed., *Alexander the Great: Selections from Arrian, Diodorus, Plutarch, and Quintus* (Indianapolis: Hackett, 2005), 156.

17. A. W. Tozer, *The Knowledge of the Holy*, 81–82.

18. This anecdote is based on a story found at http://elims.org.ua.

19. Steve Saint, "Obituary for Mincaye," ITEC, 2020, https://www.itecusa.org/mincaye.

20. https://creedboutique.com/pages/legacy.

21. This story was adapted from Jerry and Marilyn Fine, *One on One with God* (workbook and leader's guide), https://oneononewithgod.com.

22. This story was adapted from an account told on http://ntn.ua/uk.

23. This story was adapted from a story at http://pritchi.ru.

24. Michael Rydelnik and James Spencer, "Isaiah," in *The Moody Bible Commentary*, Michael Rydelnik and Michael Vanlaningham, eds. (Chicago: Moody, 2014), 1079–80.

25. This analogy from early church fathers is explained by Dr. Jonathan Sarfati at https://creation.com/trinity-analogies-countering-critics. You will also find other ways to explain the Trinity at this site. In addition, Dr. Tony Evans gives a clear description of the Trinity on pages 41–42 and 369–70 in *Theology You Can Count On* (Chicago: Moody, 2008).

26. Noël Piper, quoted in John Piper, "Thankful for the Love of God," Desiring God, November 18, 2001, https://www.desiringgod.org/messages/thankful-for-the-love-of-god.

27. Based on an article from Jonathan Pearlman, "Australians Mourn Don Ritchie - the Angel of The Gap," *Telegraph*, May 14, 2012, https://www.telegraph.co.uk/news/worldnews/australiaandthepacific/australia/9264571/Australians-mourn-Don-Ritchie-the-Angel-of-The-Gap.html.

28. Chabad.org Staff, "Texts of Blessings Before Eating," Chabad.org, https://www.chabad.org/library/article_cdo/aid/90551/jewish/Texts-of-Blessings-Before-Eating.htm.

29. Ibid.

30. Various translations have slight differences in the wording of Mark 14:22. Some can be rendered with Jesus taking the bread, blessing it, and giving thanks. How-

ever, the King James reads like this: "And as they did eat, Jesus took bread, and blessed, and brake it, and gave to them, and said, Take, eat: this is my body." In the Middle East, you can use phrases such as "bless the vine" or "bless the bread," asking someone to pray. In the context of Hebrew, however, it will always mean "Bless the *Lord*, who gave this vine," or "Bless the *Lord*, who gave this bread," and not mean "to bless" the bread or the vine itself. It's like we might say, "The ball is in your court." We're actually not talking about a ball, but we're using an idiom that means, "It's up to you now."

31. For example, *Prayers for Today: A Yearlong Journey of Devotional Prayer* by Kurt Bjorklund is filled with prayers gleaned from Scripture and from believers both contemporary and classic.

32. A. W. Tozer, *The Knowledge of the Holy*, 53.

33. W. Bingham Hunter, *The God Who Hears* (Downers Grove, IL: InterVarsity Press, 1986), 79.

CONTACT

We trust you have enjoyed and benefited from this book. We invite you to visit the website www.worshipalphabet.com and also look for us on social media.

Partners' network: www.patreon.com/worshipalphabet

Tags for this book in social media: #kitchentabledevotions #abcworship